# Dear Children . . . Love, Mom

# Dear Children . . . Love, Mom

## Joy Fay Tiner

**VANTAGE PRESS**
New York

FIRST EDITION

All rights reserved, including the right of
reproduction in whole or in part in any form.

Copyright © 2002 by Joy Fay Tiner

Published by Vantage Press, Inc.
516 West 34th Street, New York, New York 10001

Manufactured in the United States of America
ISBN: 0-533-14226-1

Library of Congress Catalog Card No.: 2002190265

0 9 8 7 6 5 4 3 2 1

# Preface

One of the things that I had to consider in writing this story is, should I be so transparent and bare my soul to the public? I concluded that if I could show that I lived my life where the rubber meets the road, so to speak, and it related to others in trying circumstances, it would mean much to me.

Everyone should know who Christ is and what He is about. He has the power to curse and make die, or to bless and make alive. He cursed the fig tree; it died. He called Lazarus back from the dead; he lived.

God created both Pharaoh and Moses. Are you a Pharaoh or a Moses? God wants us to allow him to mold our character and fashion us in his likeness and his personality.

If you could choose, would you rather be a Holy Ghost celebrity or a Hollywood celebrity with your name in lights? A Holy Ghost celebrity is someone who may or may not be known among men of this earth. In the courts of heaven, before the throne of God, Christ is proclaiming their names to the Father of lights continually.

Have you gone or are you going through great sorrow here? Is there someone or something that has offended you greatly? Does it seem as if the one offending you is winning in the circle of this life? There is another circle where God and all the Holy Angels are. When the circles of this life have turned their last twirl and it is time to give account in that heavenly circle, of the deeds done in the flesh, which will be winning then? While we breathe in this life, is the time to make things right. The heavenly Father is a merciful God. His mercies are new each morning. Let us be quick to repent, quick to forgive, and quick to be merciful ourselves.

My desire and my prayer is that this book will be a mighty tool in witnessing and winning souls for the Kingdom of God. To show also that God still makes himself known to mankind today. God is no respecter of persons. What He does for one, He will do for anyone.

As you read through the pages of this book, you will see how Jesus revealed Himself to a toddler, took that toddler at the age of three into a beautiful garden, and revealed the plan of salvation.

As Paul the apostle would say, "Grace and peace be unto all that are in Him."

# Acknowledgments

I want to acknowledge all of you who, through the years, repeatedly encouraged me to write a book. I especially want to say thank you to my husband, Carl, and also to all of our six children who encouraged me greatly. Children, you said that you wanted your children to hear and know that the God of the Word still works and breathes in real-life situations today. Carl, you said that God didn't allow me to have all these wonderful experiences in Him just to keep to myself. You have repeatedly, through the years, said that not to share them with others would be selfish. Thank you for your encouragement in this matter.

My regards to all of you.
Wife, Mother, and Friend

# 1

Dear Children, Deborah, Michael, Sherry, Carl, Darrell, and Karen, I would like to share some of my life experiences with you. Deborah, I hope that you will share these experiences with Paul and Joshua. Michael, can I count on you to share these with your children, Michele, Jennifer, Caleb, Sarah, and Josiah? Sherry, I feel certain that your children will want to hear Grandma's experiences in life. Please tell Gale (Sonnie), Shandera, Wendy, Lonnie, and Lindsey of these encounters. Carl, I know that you have told them before, but will you please tell them again to your children Tristin, Alicia, Brandon, and Nathan? Darrell, show these things to your children, Travis, Trevor, and Chaela. Karen, please tell Tiara and Tyrone of these experiences.

Children, as you each share these experiences with your children, I know that you now have experiences of your own that you can share. Tell each child to pass them on to their children. Be sure to tell of the heroes long ago. Such as the Hebrew boys in the fiery furnace, Daniel in the lion's den, David and the stone that he threw at Goliath. Giants still fall in the name of Jesus. Tell them of Peter walking on the water.

Do your children know that the God who created heaven and earth still walks among us today? Do they know that his ear is ever in tune to their prayer, that His eye roams to and fro over the earth, and that he is searching and seeking those who will follow and obey him?

Some of my earliest memories are of Jesus. Jesus showed up on a regular basis, usually daily, like a visitor dropping by, spending a lot of time with me. My days were filled with his presence. I spoke regularly to Jesus, informing my parents of His visits and conversations. Their reaction was always the same. They explained to me over and over that Jesus wasn't really in my yard today, that I only imagined that I saw Him. My sister, Murvell, who is five years older than I am, later told me that when I started walking and talking, one of my first words was "Jesus." She said no one knew how I knew about Him.

On one occasion when I was about three years old, Jesus came on one of those regular visits. On that day he took me through a white gate into a beautiful garden. We sat down on a beautiful white bench and talked. The flowers, grass, and trees were beautiful. Everything was beautiful, and the atmosphere was indescribably wonderful. There were birds that flew by, beautiful birds of various colors. Jesus seemed to know each of them personally. The birds would call His name as they flew by. With such love and tenderness, they spoke His name as they greeted Him. He in turn would return the greeting with such love and tenderness, calling them by name. I thought this only normal until I was older and realized that birds do not talk to everyone.

While in this beautiful garden, Jesus started explaining the plan of salvation to me. He explained how there is a heavenly Father called "God," how He was God's son, and how He came to this earth to die for the sins of the people. He said that He was coming again some day for all of those who believe in Him and receive Him as their Redeemer, to take them to live with Him in His home.

Jesus talked with me there in the garden for a long time; it seemed like most of the afternoon. He arose from the bench, and I arose too. He then led me back through that beautiful white gate into my own back yard. Jesus said, "It is getting late; go now into the house to your mama." I did as I was told. I hurried quickly into the house, very excited. "Mama! Come quick! Hurry, Mama! I want to show you this beautiful garden in our back yard where Jesus took me today."

Mama took my hand, and we ran quickly to the back of the house. There was no garden. Mama must have seen how surprised and disappointed that I was as my little heart exclaimed, "It's gone!" Mama didn't chide or scold me. She didn't say anything about my imagination; she in fact didn't say anything.

The next day as I was at play, Jesus came again. Again He took me back through that same white gate. We were in the same lovely garden, and we sat on the same white bench. Jesus continued explaining the plan of salvation. He then led me back through that same gate into my own back yard. He had spent most of the afternoon with me. His instructions were the same as the day before. "It is getting late," He said, "go quickly into the house to your mama." I ran fast, yelling as I went. "Mama! Mama! Run fast to the kitchen window and see that beautiful garden where Jesus took me again today." We looked out the window together, but there was no garden. Again I was disappointed and surprised. I was sure we had hurried fast enough. I so badly wanted Mama to see that beautiful garden. Again Mama didn't scold or chide. I was sure that she would see what I had seen, and she would see I wasn't just imagining this. I did not know what the word "imagination," meant exactly, I only knew that whatever a person thought happened didn't really happen if that thing called imagination was responsible.

I realize that this is quite a story to tell. I now understand why my parents thought that I was imagining all those visits from Jesus. I know now and have always known that this was not my imagination. Jesus spoke this world into existence; why can He not appear when He wants to?

I believe that this garden experience and all of the visits from Jesus were an open vision. In my studies I have read teachings that teach when a heavenly being comes and uses our earthly surroundings to show us something, that we are seeing an open vision. I do wonder if the garden was a vision of heaven.

Jesus spent two consecutive afternoons with me in the garden. On the third day, in succession, Jesus showed up again. I was on the north side of the house. Jesus walked up, took my hand, and began to walk around the yard with me. He said, "When you grow up and become a woman, will you be a missionary for me? Will you take my gospel to the world?" I replied, "Yes, I will."

That evening after our evening meal, I told Mama and Daddy. "Today Jesus asked me if I would be a missionary for Him when I grow up. I told Him I would." Mama said, "These are modern times. Jesus no longer has missionaries; that was only for Bible days long ago."

The next day at play when Jesus came, I explained, "I can't be a missionary. Mama said that you don't use missionaries today, that missionaries were only for Bible days." Jesus replied, "When you grow up, will you preach my gospel to the world?" Again I said, "Yes." Jesus never once said my mama was wrong. He just asked again in a little different manner. That evening after the evening meal, I discussed this day's conversations with my parents. Mama became very angry, "Where did you hear that word, preach my gospel?" "Jesus told me," I replied. She said nothing more to me on the matter.

I do not recall anyone coming and sharing that gospel with us. Words cannot describe how grateful I am that Jesus made himself real to me. I know that Christ is alive. He is who He says, the Son of God, and He is soon to appear on the scene before all mankind. I have no idea in the scope of time, but it can't be long. We must all be ready to have the wedding garments on without spot or wrinkle. I believe that the trumpet could sound at any moment and the Bride of Christ will be gone. Are you ready? I want to share a dream with you that I had when I was four years old.

I had an older sister, Jessie. She was the same age as my mother, only eleven months younger. She was my dad's daughter, and she was very precious. She and her husband J.D. came to visit us on the farm regularly. They always did many nice things for us kids. They didn't have children. Once when they came to visit, Jessie said the next time that she came she would bring some beautiful blue ribbons for my hair. "Wouldn't Fay look pretty with two blue ribbons in that pretty black curly hair?" she said to my mother. I couldn't think of anything else. Night and day my mind and my heart were on those ribbons. I wanted them so badly. Jesus would come in His usual manner on a regular basis. I didn't have time for Him. I was too busy thinking about those ribbons and wishing that Jessie would hurry and come back. I would spurn Jesus away. I would fall asleep thinking about those ribbons and awaken with them on my mind. Oh, how I yearned to have them. I no longer had time for Jesus.

Weeks went by, and one night I had a dream. I dreamed that Jesus came in a train that was flying through the air. He was picking up people who loved Him and were ready to go when He came. He stopped at our farm, picked us up, and was flying to the next farm where the Johnsons lived. I was seated in the front seat and Jesus kept looking at me. I had two BIG beautiful blue ribbons on either side of my head. Jesus said, "You will have to decide what you want the most, Me or those ribbons. You can't go live with Me in My home with those ribbons in your hair. You must decide before I make my next stop."

I hated to part with my ribbons, but I didn't want to live anywhere apart from Jesus. I threw the ribbons out of the window. Jesus stopped for the neighbors, and we sailed off into the heavens. I awoke. Jessie never brought the ribbons. I no longer desired them because I wanted Jesus first. Ribbons are not sinful, but I allowed them to become sinful to me because I allowed them to be more important to me than fellowshipping with Jesus. I sometimes cry when I think of that dream and how foolishly I behaved over ribbons. I am thankful that God can reach into the heart of a four-year-old and reveal sin. Fellowship was restored and Jesus continued to visit me on that farm.

Mama and Daddy continued to tell me it was not so, and that my imagination was at work. They would tell me I could not believe that I was really seeing Jesus because I was not, and that I could not go on like that. I was now about five years old. The very next day after this kind but long lecture, guess who came to visit with me? That's right, it was Jesus. We took each other's hands and began to walk over the yard as usual. *Today is the day,* I thought, *now is the time. I must be done with this imagination business once and for all.* I trusted Mama and Daddy to know what they were talking about.

"Jesus, I can't believe that you are really here. Mama and Daddy say that it is only my imagination and that I must stop it." "Do you see me?" Jesus asked. "I do see you,"

I replied. "Do you believe that I am here?" He asked. "I know that you are here," I said. Jesus never once said that my parents were wrong. He just proved Himself real. It was not my imagination.

The last time that I recall seeing Jesus on that old home place was when I was six, almost seven, in the beginning of spring. I was out at play as usual; Jesus walked up beside me and began talking. He said, "Look as far as your eye can see in that direction," as he pointed his finger. "Farther than your eye can see is California. Your brother Bill is coming soon to move you to California." I said, "I know that you are wrong this time, Jesus. I don't even have a brother named Bill." I ran quickly into the house. "Mama, do I have a brother Bill?" I wanted to know. "Yes, you do," she said. "Where is he?" I asked. "In California," she replied. "Is he coming soon to move us to California?" I asked. "No," she answered. "Jesus told me my brother Bill was coming soon to move me to California."

A short time after Jesus told me that I was moving to California, my dad took the cream from the farm to Marietta to market. This was a regular happening on the farm. Today would be different. Dad came home at his usual time from one of these trips. Mama had dinner waiting. Being more jovial than usual, Dad was rehearsing the events of the day as we sat around the table. He was not a religious man, but he stated that he believed that the signs of the times indicated that Jesus would soon return to this earth. At that moment he lost consciousness and his head fell into his plate. A medical exam revealed that Dad had had a stroke.

My mother informed Daddy's older children of his physical condition. His daughter Jessie, in Texas, and the two sons in California. Bill made an immediate response to my parents. His letter stated, "Dad, sell everything that you cannot get into the back of my car. I will be there in a few days. I will stay a week and I will bring you and the family back to California so I can keep an eye on you."

Shortly after our arrival in Bakersfield, California, my twin, Troy, and I had our seventh birthday. Jesus knew that I had a brother Bill, but I didn't know that I did. Jesus knows all things. I repent that I told Jesus that He was wrong about that. Jesus is never wrong about anything.

Our new dwelling place was now in a place called Bakersfield. Bakersfield is located in the San Joaquin Valley. Many people who live in this valley get "valley fever." Valley fever can be fatal since there is no cure for it. Soon after our arrival in this valley, I became one of the many. By fall I had a severe case of valley fever. The doctors told my parents that it was one of the worst cases of valley fever that they had ever seen. They informed Mom and Dad that I couldn't live long. They said that if my parents would take me out of the valley, that I could only live a short time longer.

Mom and Dad planned, packed, and set the alarm for five o'clock the next morning. They wanted to get an early start over the grapevine into Los Angeles. When the alarm went off, they got up as they had planned. They were undecided as to what to do. I overheard them discussing this matter. Dad said, "We can't be sure that she will live any longer if we leave here. We don't know anyone there. Let's just stay here. If she lives, she lives. If she dies, she dies." So stay we did. I never told my folks that I heard their discussion. I believe that they made the right choice. I will explain later in another chapter how God miraculously healed me of valley fever after I was grown.

I no longer had visits from Jesus as I did when I was a little girl on the farm. I did have a sweet relation with him, knowing that he was present at all times. I wasn't afraid of dying. I didn't have any thoughts or plans of dying. I was too weak to get out of bed by myself. Mama and Murvell got on either side of me, helping me in and out of bed. That ordeal lasted almost four months. I gradually grew stronger. The day came when I could get out of bed by myself. I got strong enough that I could go outside and be up longer.

One warm spring day, I was standing out in the driveway enjoying the fresh air and the sunshine. I was turning my arms up in order to let the warm sunshine touch my skin. It felt so wonderful! "Thank you, Jesus," I said, "for this good sunshine, for the privilege to be outside, and for the strength to stand." At that moment I realized that I had never invited Jesus into my heart. "Jesus," I said, "I don't know if I am old enough to ask you into my heart. If I am old enough, will you please come into my heart? Jesus, someone, somewhere once told me that no one is born saved, that everyone must invite you into his or her heart. So please, Jesus, come into my heart and save my soul. Thank you, amen."

What ecstasy, what joy spread over and through me. I've never regretted that moment when I asked Jesus into my heart. He truly is that friend who sticketh closer than a brother. The many times that I saw Jesus and talked with Him as a child, didn't save my soul. I still had to give Him the invitation.

I praise God that He allowed Jesus to reveal Himself to me. I know that Christ is alive; He is who He says that He is. This millennium will reveal to all mankind, even to Satan, that He is that Eternal King who is to come and set up His kingdom.

Children, we do not need to wait for that millennium kingdom or heaven to allow Jesus to be the Lord of our lives. He has been fighting battles for mankind since time began. He will fight your battles for you just as He did for

Joshua and the children of Israel. Let me remind you of Joshua 5:13–15; "And it came to pass, when Joshua was by Jericho, that he lifted up his eyes and looked, and behold, there stood a man over against him with his sword drawn in his hand. And Joshua went unto him and said unto him, 'Art thou for us or for our adversaries?' And he said 'Nay, but as captain of the host of the Lord am I now come.' And Joshua fell on his face to the earth, and did worship and said unto him, 'What saith my Lord unto His servant?' And the captain of the Lord's host said unto Joshua, 'Loose thy shoe from off thy foot, for the place whereon thou standest is holy.' And Joshua did so."

The captain of the host of the Lord will fight your battles. You may not see him with your physical eyes as Joshua did, or you may see Him (as God chooses).

I want you to know and realize that God the Father, God the Son, and God the Holy Spirit are always with you if you belong to Jesus and are washed in His precious blood. He says in His Word a number of times, "I will never leave thee nor forsake thee. Lo, I am with thee always, even unto the end of the world. I will never fail thee."

# 2

Joshua was faithful to obey God's commands, receive instruction, and follow after righteousness. He crossed the Jordan and headed for the Promised Land as he was instructed. The captain of the Lord's host showed up to fight for Him.

Children, when you, I, or anyone serves God, and crosses the Jordan in our life in obedience in all that God asks of us, the captain of the Lord's host will be there to help us win our battles. The captain of the Lord's host is none other than "Jesus Christ Himself." The very Son of God. Let us remember this as we journey to the Promised Land (heaven).

I have much more that I want to share with you. I trust that through it all, you will take note that it is the triune God who intercepts the enemy's strategies, sometimes performing the supernatural in order to bring victory.

First of all, my dear ones, read, study, and apply the Word of God in your daily life. I admonish you with all diligence to please do so. The good Holy Bible is our road map to heaven, the guide through this life. The Bible teaches us how to live and how to die. It has such wonderful words of instruction, wisdom, strength, courage, etc. God's Word is truth. If anything is contrary to God's Word, please don't receive it. The Bible is the only book that is alive. It is quick, powerful, and sharper than any two-edged sword, piercing even to the dividing asunder of soul and spirit and of the joints and marrow, and it is a discerner of the thoughts and intents of the heart (Hebrews 4:12).

Let me share an experience concerning: THE BIBLE, THE WORD OF GOD.

We came home from service one evening and I was tired. I decided to go to my room to lie down and rest awhile before getting the children ready for bed. I fell into a little dream, trance, revelation; I'm not sure what to call it. It was a scenario. I do know that God revealed something to me through this little scenario. In this scenario, I was at our church in the Women's Missionary Room with a group of ladies. I had my Bible on my lap. Suddenly my Bible was slipping and falling to the floor. I felt very grieved and brokenhearted to think that I was so careless with it. As it was falling, I heard my Bible say, "Uh, oh!" I caught it with my feet. I didn't know what the ladies might think about my Bible talking to me. Quickly I looked embarrassedly around. No one seemed to have noticed. I was relieved. I looked back at my Bible. I said, "You spoke, who are you?" To my surprise it answered, "I'm the Bible, the Word of God."

The scene then changed and I saw billions of books on bookshelves all over the world. I saw a book coming down off of one of the top shelves. It was my Bible; it was speaking as it was coming down. It said, "Of all the books that has ever been written since the beginning of time, I am the only book that is alive and is able to come down off the shelf and speak to anyone, anywhere, any hour of the day or night." The vision ended. I was back in my room lying on my bed.

I quickly got up in search of my Bible. It wasn't on the dresser or the chest. I went into the dining room; it wasn't on the table or the piano. Looking through into the living room, I saw it wasn't on the mantel. I looked around the corner, and there it was, lying on the bookshelf. At that moment my entire being flooded with mixed emotions. I wanted to grab that precious book and hug it to me, and at the same time, I wanted to jump back and exclaim, "That thing is alive."

I treasure this experience. No devil would have shown me such a scenario. He wouldn't want me, or anyone, to realize how alive and how true the written Word of God is. If you recall when Jesus was forty days in the wilderness, being tempted of the devil, he defeated Satan with the Word. Jesus would always reply to Satan "it is written" and quote the Scripture to him. You can find this in the fourth chapter of Luke.

There are scoffers who scoff at the Holy Word of God. That doesn't make it any less true. You can follow its instructions. It will lead you into the ark of safety.

Scoffers scoffed at Noah, but by the instructions and plan of God, Noah built an ark to save man and beast alive. Man's wisdom built the *Titanic*, but it sank. I'm sure that it was a masterpiece, but not indestructible. Praise God for man's wisdom and all that our heavenly Father allows mankind to accomplish. But in comparison to God's wisdom, there is no comparison.

Stick with the Word of God and don't be short-changed. We now have versions of the Bible that leave out the Virgin Birth, the blood, and other important issues. Those are nothing more than just another book on a shelf. Children, it is urgent that you do not get a road map to heaven with all or part of the map removed. Your eternal destiny depends on it.

I now have explained how Jesus revealed himself alive to me at a very young age. I explained how the Bible, the Word of God, revealed itself alive to me when I was a young woman. There is something else that is just as real as Jesus the Son of God and just as real as the Bible, the Word of

God. Jesus is the Word. That something else is the supernatural work of God.

A number of years ago, I began to have some problems with my stomach. I had terrible stomach pains that enveloped my entire being. It could last for days. Medication helped temporarily. One Sunday after a church service, I was walking in the fellowship hall and one of these attacks hit. The Lord began to speak to me. He said that people as a whole tend to live in the natural realm. "Many say they believe in me, but they keep me way out in space. When you get a cold, you say that it is only natural or a common cold. You say that you know that I exist and that I can do anything, but you keep Me at a distance, never inviting Me into your circumstance or situation. You say that it is only natural. Don't you know that when you bring Me into your 'Now,' that the natural becomes supernatural?"

A light went on in my understanding. I, at that moment, asked Jesus to heal my stomach condition. I was healed instantly. A year later I was walking in the family room. One of those attacks tried to hit. I grabbed my stomach and started to say, "Oh, no," when suddenly I remembered that I was healed. "Satan," I said, "you can't put this back on me. Jesus healed me last year." That reprimand was twenty years ago. I have never had another one of those attacks.

I have spoken to you about Jesus, The Word, and the supernatural. Before I go further with my own experiences, may I share another incident that involves another pastor and his family? I will avoid revealing names and places.

There was as pastor whom we will call "Pastor X." He and his family were pastoring a church about thirty-five miles from us. One day someone handed him a card that said, "Expect a Miracle." Pastor X thought, as he went on his way, *I don't need a miracle,* and he tossed the little card in the trash. He felt prompted to go back and get the little card. That very day he needed a miracle. His young daughter didn't make it home from school at her usual time.

The school bus stop was only a few feet from where Pastor X and his family lived; yet there was danger. When the little girl got off the bus, two strangers grabbed her and threw her into their car. No one saw this, or so it seemed, but God was watching. You do recall that I told you that God's eye is on the sparrow and he watches over you. When these men started to leave the main highway and start up a mountain road, they had a flat tire. Some folks stopped to help; the men became concerned now that someone had seen them who could identify them. They took Pastor X's daughter back and dropped her off a few feet from her house.

The folks who had helped with the flat tire heard the news; there was an all-points bulletin for those men. They realized that these were the same two men and were able to be beneficial in helping the authorities to locate the men. Those men had abducted little girls at other places and their fate was not as good as was Pastor X's daughter. The report was that they always molested and mutilated the little girls.

# 3

You children have heard me say many times that if you belong to God, you cant' go under for going over. Even if you do go down in death, you do not go down in defeat. You just go over to the other side if you have been washed in the blood of Jesus and your sins are washed away.

Know that, dear ones, even as Jesus stood up and cried "Peace be still," as the storm was beating on the disciples and their ship that day with the waves raging high, he still has power over the wind and waves. You may be facing a storm in your life of a different type. It may seem as if it will take your little lifeboat under. Jesus can calm the raging winds of adversity in your life. We must be like the three Hebrew boys whom the king had thrown into the fiery furnace.

They said, "Our God is able to deliver us, O King, but whether he does or whether he doesn't, what is that to us?" In essence, they were saying we do not belong to ourselves. We belong to God and it is none of our business what he allows for us.

Throughout the years, and to this very day, Jesus continues to talk to me on a regular basis, the same as he does with all of you who belong to Him. However, upon my leaving the farm, Jesus did not show up in the same manner so that I could see with my natural eye. That has only happened on special occasions that I will share later. Jesus speaks to His people in numerous ways. First he speaks through His Word, the Bible, through that still small voice, through the word of knowledge, one of the nine gifts of the Spirit. He speaks through dreams, visions, revelations, etc. Let me share just such a vision with you.

I was ten years old and in the fifth grade when I saw this vision in complete detail. I have no knowledge of where I was at when I saw this. I believe that I must have been at school in class, because I came home from school with it so pressed in my memory that I began to question my mother about it.

Wherever I was at, I was momentarily not there but in another place at a school called Greeley. I was in the fifth grade. Our teacher was Ms. Miller, with red hair and glasses. She was very petite and very nice. She was also the teacher of the sixth grade. This school was so small that one teacher taught two grades in one room. I saw some of the students there and knew them by name. The vision was so impressed on me for many days to the point that each day when I came home from school I would ask my mother if we were moving to a placed called Greeley. Her reply was always the same. "I don't know of a place called Greeley."

But still I continued to question her each day. In looking back, I wonder how she kept herself from becoming irritated at my asking the same question over and over, relating the same scenario in minute detail. Two or three weeks after the vision, my dad's job on a construction project ended. My brother Ovalee invited my dad to move onto some of his property and work on his ranch. Guess what?! We were enrolled in a school called Greeley.

On the first day of school, there was a girl named Christine who offered to show me around and introduce me to some of the students. She was amazed to see that I already knew some of them by name. "This is Charles," she said. "I know. Where is his twin Robert?" I replied. In amazement she said, "Have you been here before?" "No," I said. "How do you know them by name?" she asked. The bell rang and it was time to go to class. The matter was dropped and never came up again.

Soon after our moving to this new place, the pastor of the community church began to pick us up and take us to church. My parents went too. I certainly enjoyed the services and the Sunday school. Our teacher was so concerned about us and so interested in us that she made a lasting impression on me. Our pastor was a woman. She was very anointed, and very caring, and she made an even greater impression on me.

I began to seek for the "baptism of the Holy Spirit." I sought diligently for two or three months. It was now summertime; Mama and Daddy were gone all day to work. Siblings, Wesley, Troy, and Odean played out in the woods all day. I cleaned house each morning as quickly as I could so that I could go to my place of prayer and seek for the baptism. In the evening before Mama, Daddy, and Murvell came home, I would start dinner so that it would be ready to put on the table. I cooked on a wooden cook stove. What a life! We didn't feel neglected or rejected. We felt useful and happy to be a part of family living.

When at church, I continued to seek for the baptism. One Sunday morning I waited until all of the ladies were in the ladies' prayer room, then very quietly I entered the prayer room. I did not want the ladies to be aware of my presence. They knew how hungry I was for the baptism. They too were very desirous that I receive that heavenly language. I thought that they probably had dinner in the oven and I did not want anyone's roast to burn. I would just sneak quietly in and out of the prayer room. All that I wanted to do was kneel and tells Jesus "I love you," then sneak quietly away. But that night I was coming back there and I was not leaving until I received the filling of the Holy Spirit. I was unaware of the glory and the ecstasy that awaited me.

"Jesus, I love you," I said as I knelt in prayer. At that instant I entered another dimension. I heard a sound as of a mighty rushing wind, fell into a trance, unaware of time or anyone or thing around me. Somewhere, off in the distance, I heard the most beautiful heavenly language that I've ever heard in my life. I began a gradual return to my natural surroundings. The language got closer and closer. Lo and behold! That was me, that was me. I was speaking in a heavenly language. I'd received my baptism in the Spirit. I was ten years old and I did not know that on the day of Pentecost, when the one hundred and twenty were in the upper room, that was when the Holy Spirit was poured out. It came as a sound, as a mighty rushing wind. I praise God for that wonderful experience. Everyone doesn't have this kind of experience. Each one receives differently. The next summer I was baptized in water.

Children, by now you may be thinking that I was a sweet little angel. Let me set the record straight. By now I was a complete tomboy, rowdy and loud mouthed, full of life, with plans to live life to the fullest. Although I was still of the above, I respected my parents, my teachers, elderly, and all others. I tried never to infringe on others people's rights, time, or property. Because of my mother's illness, we didn't have training like other children. I am sure that my behavior gave people the wrong impression of me. I was very honest and open. Dad taught us kids that if we lied, cheated, or stole, he would kill us.

Now remember, he was not religious until later in life. He would not have harmed us, for he was very kind. I recall getting only one spanking from him in all of my life. We thought that he would kill us or make us wish that we were dead. Daddy always took me on his lap and began his lecture by saying, "Now, Fay. . . ." By this time my little heart was broken into a million pieces because I'd done something against Dad's wishes or instruction. "You know that you should not have done that," he would continue. He was so kind and wonderful; it just broke my heart to displease him. If he would have given me a good spanking, I think that I would have thought that I paid my debt to society and I could do it again. Because of his kindness and the way that he took me on his lap and with tender patience instructed me, I just wanted to please him and do things right.

That is how our heavenly Father is. He deals with us in such tender mercies. God does have a wrathful side for the wicked and rebellious. My rowdiness only lasted for a couple of years. I met my future husband when I was thirteen, shortly before my fourteenth birthday. I had to grow up and be ladylike in a quick hurry. I did not want him to see me as a tomboy. One of his sisters thought that perhaps he should not become interested in me because she thought that I was too feisty.

I enjoyed sports and was very involved in them. I stopped the sports that I was involved in when I met Carl, who would later be my husband.

There was a new church starting up in the area. My mother visited there and saw this very nice looking boy. One day she said, "Joy, there is a very nice looking boy over at this new church that I would like for you to meet." I could not let Mom know that I was the least bit interested in checking this out. I said something like, "So what! Who cares!" And I continued in softball for another couple of weeks, pretending that I couldn't care less, knowing in my heart that when the time was right and Mom had enough time to forget that it was her idea, I would check this matter out.

Check it out I did. I talked Ielene, my friend, into going to that church with me one Sunday morning. Wow! Sitting there on the platform was a very handsome young man, playing his guitar in the orchestra and singing. I had never seen anyone like that in all of my life. He later sang a special. Could he ever sing! He seemed so in love with Jesus. My heart was racing so fast and doing flip-flops all at the same time. I said, "Lord, if you were ever to give me anything like that for a husband, I would just never quit praising you." This young man invited me to the ice-cream social that was prepared for the youth. I accepted the invitation. We courted for the next two years and then were married. We have now been married for fifty years.

While we were courting, Carl took me to the county fair. Our friends were all getting their fortunes told and they would come out with all these exciting stories to tell about the future. I wanted to get my fortune told also, so pay the fare I did, but the little Gypsy lady just looked at me and said, "I cannot tell your fortune." At that time I was disappointed. I thought that I had been cheated. I know now that fortune-telling is of the devil. I'm glad that she couldn't tell my fortune. She did tell me that I was a very fortunate young lady.

When Carl and I got married, we were both very young. We had no one to help us plan a wedding, to send invitations, or anything that goes with a wedding. My dad was then paralyzed from strokes, and he could not give me away. Two ignorant kids planning and preparing their wedding. I should say we did not plan or prepare, we just got married. The church was packed even though we did not send out one invitation.

Wesley, my brother, thought that we were both too

young and that the responsibilities would be too great. Moments before the wedding, he tried to talk me out of getting married. He said that he had tickets and we could just leave. My brother is precious and wise, and I was giving ear to him. Suddenly I realized that the wedding march had started over for the third time. I jumped out of the car and ran halfway down the aisle before I remembered that I was supposed to be marching down the aisle.

We wanted children desperately. We had been married several months when I decided to go to the doctor to see why I was not expecting a baby. The doctor, after examining me, said that I would never have children because I didn't have anything to carry a baby in. I had had a severe injury just prior to my seventh birthday, before I moved to California. Now I was told that I had no womb.

That evening Carl and I knelt in prayer and asked God for a baby. Ten months later Deborah was born. It was not just that easy. Remember, children, at the beginning of this story, I told you that I had valley fever for which there is no cure. Unbeknownst to me, I now had encephalitis, known as sleeping sickness. I later learned that there were about four hundred people in that county who had this sleeping sickness. A mosquito carried it. I lost weight instead of gaining weight. Finally I gained five pounds. When the baby was born, she weighed four pounds and fifteen ounces. Three hours before I went into labor, my best friend's mother suggested that I see another doctor. She said I probably only had a small tumor and wasn't pregnant at all.

The labor was a long one due to all the complications. I was in a hospital where no one could be present with you. My husband couldn't be there; my mother couldn't be there. I was not aware at this time that I had sleeping sickness nor did I know that I had a kidney infection and that my blood pressure was very high. I did know that I was very sick.

Hour after excruciating hour went by, without any success. I began to realize that something was wrong. I began to lose consciousness. When I regained consciousness, I could not remember who I was or where I was. Once when I regained consciousness, Jesus was standing by my bed in a white robe. He was holding my hand. In His presence I knew who I was and that I was dying. I remembered that the summer when I was fifteen Jesus had asked me to have some teenage meetings to win souls for the kingdom of God. I didn't know how, and besides, who wanted to hear a girl preach? I did not obey, now I lay dying.

"Jesus, if you will heal my body, I will preach your gospel. I will go where you want me to go and I will do what you want me to do," I said. Later a nurse came, found me, and screamed for help. I was in shock and having convulsions. They took me to the delivery room and began to work on me. I didn't know that when you are dying, they beat you up to keep you alive. They began slapping my face very hard. Once they were beating me in the chest with their fists. *What have I done to anger them so?* I wondered, not realizing that they were doing this for my own good.

When I entered the delivery room, I saw a brilliant bright light coming down out of the ceiling. It was so bright that these natural eyes could not look at it. It was like staring at the sun. I thought, *This must be a light to sterilize everything.* I later realized that it was the presence of the Lord.

My soul began to leave my body, but I didn't know that was what was happening. I thought that the nurses and the doctor were hoisting me to the ceiling with some type of hoist. Before my soul left my body, Satan came to me. He looked like a big snake in the form of a man. Satan said,

"You don't need to believe in God. When you die, you are just dead, no life after death." My spirit cried out, "Satan, you're a liar!" He then tried a different approach. He said, "It won't do you any good to believe in God because before he was, I was, and I am greater than God is." Again my spirit cried out, "Satan, you are a liar!" Children, the devil will try to the very last to damn your soul to hell. Keep that helmet of salvation at all times. I could not think for myself, but my spirit knew and cried out for me.

When my soul left my body, all of my senses went with me. I was up in the ceiling in a corner, looking down, watching them work with me. Slapping my face and chest. I said to myself, "They do not know that I am up here, because they cannot see me." I watched until they pulled the sheet over my head. Then my soul went through the ceiling like it wasn't even there. It was twenty minutes till 2:00 A.M.

In the darkness of the hour, I could see the silhouette of the trees and buildings that surrounded the hospital. My brother Wesley was three floors down, fighting for his life at that very moment. His appendix was ruptured. Neither of us knew that the other one was there.

I continue on my journey through space until I come to a mountain ridge. I float right over the top of the mountains, landing on my feet in a valley. I realize that I am a long way from planet Earth and I am all alone. I am unafraid; I have no fear and no pain. The valley is very dusky dark. I can hardly see my hand in front of my face. I can feel warm sand under my feet. I walk until I reach the center of the valley, walking eastward.

Then I turn and start walking northward. I see a line of trees running from east to west and beyond those trees is such black darkness. I do not know what is there. I see a man standing under one of the trees. He has on a royal blue robe. It is Jesus. Now I realize that these trees are on the bank of a river. The river is so black that you cannot see to the other side. I know that Jesus is going to reach not one hand but two hands and lead me across that river. For a brief second, I was concerned what would happen, when we stepped into the river.

Immediately I knew that it didn't matter what happened. Jesus was walking with me, so if we walked on the bottom, on top, or somewhere in between, it didn't matter. We would reach the other side. We did walk on top of the water. When we reached the other side, Jesus just disappeared. Now I've left the realm of darkness and I've entered the sphere of brightness. It is that sphere where the Lamb is the light. I'm traveling through space again.

I said to myself, "In Sunday school, they said that there was heaven up here somewhere. If it is any more wonderful than this, it must surely be wonderful. I don't care if I never quit traveling through space." No sooner had I thought about heaven than I looked up and saw it. A golden city sitting on a hill in the northeast. I immediately floated right up to it. My left elbow rubbed against the fence of that city. It was at that moment that I realized that there was a fence around that city. I could hear people in there. They were singing and shouting and praising God. Oh! I couldn't wait to get in there. I wanted to join in the praise. I saw a gate and I said, "I guess that is the gate where I go in down there." I floated up to the gate. I reached with my right hand to open that gate, but I didn't get to touch the gate. The gate opened and out stepped Jesus. "Not yet," he said.

He then began to question me, not because He needed answers. He questioned me in order for my heart to arrive at the right conclusion. "Do you want to go in there?" he asked. He knew that I wanted in there. He knows our thoughts and he has every hair of our head numbered. "Yes," I answered.

"Do you remember that back on earth you have a husband and that you are about to deliver a child?" "No," I said. "The only thing that I know is that I was me, and I was there. I came from somewhere and now I wanted to go into this wonderful place." He allowed me to remember that I was from earth, that I had a husband and was about to deliver a child. I remembered also that the communist scare was on. That I had prayed if I should die and the child lived, please God let someone raise my baby to know the full gospel.

He said, "Do you want to go back to earth and raise your baby or do you want to go in?" I said, "I want to go in. If you want me to go back to earth to raise my baby, I will. You know if I would go back to earth and turn away from you and never stand here at these gates again. Jesus, if that would happen, take me now while I am here and I am ready." Jesus said, "It will be harder for you than it ever was before, but I will keep you."

With that, Jesus just disappeared and I started traveling through space, back to earth. Before I share the trip back down to earth, let me share some of my feelings while standing at the gates of heaven. First of all, you would think that there would be no disappointment standing at the gates of heaven. When Jesus stepped out of those gates and said, "Not yet," I knew that meant it was not time, that I would have to go back. I knew disappointment because I wanted to be in His presence to love and worship Him. I so badly wanted to remain in His presence that I did not want to go back to earth to raise all the babies that ever were born from Cain to the very last one born. There is something about being in His presence and wanting to do His will no matter what. That is why I said, "If you want me to go back,

I will go back." I was amazed that the brightness of his robe reached from horizon to horizon, as far as the eye could see, yet I could stand next to him and look into his wonderful face. Now I understand what the Scripture means when it says that the Lamb is the light of that city.

# 4

On the journey back to earth, I did not have to cross the black river or that valley. I traveled through space in the brightness where the Lamb is the light. When I entered earth's stratosphere, there was darkness because it was about four-thirty in the morning and the sun had not come up. Again I could see the silhouette of the trees and the buildings around the hospital. My soul went through the roof of the hospital as though it wasn't even there. When my soul reentered my body, it felt like lying down on the bed on my back because that was the position that my body was in. I could still see in the spirit realm for many hours after this experience. For instance, I still had the sheet over my head, but I could see straight through it. The doctor was holding the baby by the heels. She was dark purple, no sign of life. I heard the doctor say, "This baby isn't going to live either." It had been over two and one half hours. I could see the clock, it had been almost two hours and forty-five minutes. I whispered a prayer. I said, "Jesus, let my baby live." Debbie immediately cried out. The doctor pulled the sheet from over my head, got down in my face, and said, "What did you say?!" in a coarse whisper. I thought, *Oh, no, he is still angry with me.* He wasn't angry; he was scared because dead people don't talk. They called for my husband to come. Debbie and I were placed on the critical list; they didn't think that we would make it.

I was still going in and out of consciousness. I wanted

to be rational and alert when my husband arrived. I didn't want him to see me as I was. I prayed, "Father, in Jesus name, let me be conscious and alert when my husband gets here." I did not even whisper this prayer. I only thought it in my heart. When I whispered the prayer for my baby to live, that brought the doctor in my face.

When Carl drove into the parking lot, I could see him driving in because, as I stated earlier, I could see in the spirit many hours after. I saw every step he took. I watched as he climbed all three flights of stairs. When he stepped out on the floor where I was I immediately was back to reality. I prayed another prayer in my heart. I thought, *Jesus, let Carl go see the baby and go home.* He said, "I think I will go see the baby and go home." Being young he did not realize the seriousness of our condition. I spent five days, as was customary in those days. They wanted me to stay longer and then be flown to San Francisco to a specialist for surgery so I could never have another baby. I had my mother sign me out so I could go home. My gynecologist told me that I could wait six months, and when I turned eighteen, he would do the surgery and I could sign for it myself. I began asking God for a son. I hid from doctors so they couldn't discuss surgery with me. When I went back to my doctor six months later, I was expecting a son and it was too late for surgery.

I had not told Carl about my experience of dying and standing at the gates of heaven. I was afraid that he would have me committed somewhere as insane. Every day the spirit prompted me to tell him of my experience. Every day I told the Lord that tomorrow I would tell him, but I could never get the courage. One day when Debbie was almost four months old, I decided that this would be the day. We had moved sixty miles out of town on an oil lease for a company that Carl worked for. We had been to Bakersfield and had to drive the sixty miles home. I waited until we were almost home, and then I told him. If he were going to have me committed, he would have to drive the sixty miles back to town, was my reasoning. He was elated. "Why did you not tell me sooner?" he asked. "I was afraid that you would think that I was crazy," I said.

In answer to prayer, I then was expecting a son. The devil tormented me on a daily basis, several times a day. The enemy would perch on my left shoulder and he would say, "Aren't you stupid! Last year you died giving birth to one baby, now you are going to die this year and you won't come back. You will leave two babies behind with no one to raise them. Aren't you stupid!"

Momentarily such horrible fear of leaving the babies behind would sweep over me with such torment. Jesus would then come and whisper in my right ear, "I gave you back your life last year. I will give it back this year." All fear always left when Jesus spoke to me. The enemy continued to come on a regular basis to torment me. Jesus was always faithful to come and comfort me. He is faithful and greater than the enemy. The triune God is more powerful than any enemy. Please don't ever forget that. He is the one with the power to carry you from earth to glory if you have been washed in the blood of the Lord Jesus Christ, known as the Lamb of God.

One night a strange thing happened. Carl was in bed sound asleep. I prepared and came to bed later. Immediately after I got into bed, I heard the back door open. We never locked the back door, so I assumed that a prowler must have stepped in. I thought, *No fear, Carl is a man mountain* (so he was called). I'll wake him up and whoever came in here will be more than glad to get out. I tried to shake Carl; I couldn't reach him. The steps were coming closer. I tried to pinch Carl; still I couldn't reach him. The steps were coming closer and closer. I heard the steps as they came through the kitchen, through the living room, and into the hall. I looked down the hall and, *Oh, no!* I thought to myself. I immediately began applying the blood of Jesus. What I saw I had never seen before in my life.

There, coming towards me was a large beautiful being. It was not the Jesus that I knew. I kept applying the blood of Jesus, but it was not afraid of the blood of Jesus. He would not leave, he just kept coming into our bedroom. I made a final attempt to kick Carl to wake him up. It was useless; I was unable to touch him. To say that I was scared spitless would be putting it mildly. I wished that I could just die instantly. This creature looked to be about seven feet high and about three feet wide. His hair was a beautiful golden copper. It reached halfway between his knee and ankle. Magnificent beyond words, concept, or measure is the only way to describe this heavenly being. He wore dark brown sandals on his feet. When he entered our room, he went straight to Deborah's crib. I tried to scoot as close to the edge of the bed as I could so that I could fall out of bed. I wanted to crawl over to that being and flog at him in an effort to keep him away from my baby. I was not permitted to move. I couldn't even fall out of bed.

With his hand he brushed the hair back from Debbie's forehead, bent and kissed her on the forehead. With the left hand still on her head, he raised his right hand to heaven and called God the Father and blessed her for a long time. I thought, *What right do you have to call God the Father? He is my Father. I don't know who you are.* When the blessing of Debbie was completed, he then went over to our closet and took one of my maternity smock tops. Holding it in a stretched-out manner, he looked it up and down, looked over at me, and said, "You are going to have a baby." I said, "I know that." He said, "You are going to have a boy." I said,

"I know that." I thought, *I do?* He said, "You are going to call him Michael." I said, "I know that." He then came and stood at the foot of my bed. I was permitted to move. I grabbed the covers and threw them over my head. This was to no avail. I could see straight through them as though they didn't exist. I then saw a picture of a mother giving birth. The baby was buttocks first, and it was a boy. I saw the doctor lay him on something. He was crying his lungs out. I heard the words, "Mother and baby are fine." With that the being and vision were gone.

I will try to explain my conversation with that being. When he looked at my smock top, he was conveying, "I know that you are with child. The clothes you wear even declare it." I agreed with everything that he stated. First of all, I agreed with him because my spirit bore witness with truth. Secondly, I agreed with him because I was probably fearful to disagree. He spoke the truth, and I had no need to disagree. When he proclaimed that I was going to have a boy, I readily agreed. My human reasoning or sense thought, *I do! Do I really know that? . . .* But I believed the messenger. Carl and I had planned that we would name our first son Michael after the Archangel in heaven. I knew when I saw the mother giving birth and it was a boy, that it was me and my son. I knew that this would be a breech delivery.

I was so afraid of the presence of this creature that I would have been happy to die. I had goose bumps on top of goose bumps, and those bumps had their own personal bumps. I thought because I was so fearful that this was surely something evil from Satan. I never felt any evil the entire time. Since I thought that it was evil, I could not understand why it did not leave when the blood of Jesus was applied. No evil can stand when the name and blood of Jesus are applied. I've read in the Word where John and others fell down as dead when they saw an angel.

After the encounter I knew that I would have a breech delivery. I began to tell friends and relatives, "I'm going to have a breech birth." I forgot to tell you that in those days the ultra-sound had not been invented. I had no way of knowing the gender of the child. The morning following this incident, I knew that I had to tell someone, but who? What if that someone decided that I was crazy and decided to have me checked out for insanity? Still, I knew that I must tell someone. I couldn't keep this to myself. I decided to tell my husband's mother. She would probably think I was crazy, but she would keep my secret. I told Mom first thing that morning, before anything else. I said, "Mom, I had an awful experience last night." And I related everything to her in minute detail. "Joy! You saw an angel." "No, Mom, I was so scared it must have been something from hell." Three weeks later, Michael was born. Guess what?! That's right, he was born frank breech, screaming his lungs out and we were both okay.

Michael's birth was a difficult one. I had been in labor for thirty plus hours. My strength was almost gone. I said, "Lord, if you don't let me deliver in the next few minutes, I won't be here." The Lord spoke in an urgent tone and said, "No, pray to the Father in my name in the next few seconds." I said, "Father, in the name of Jesus, let me deliver in the next few seconds or I won't be here." The next thing I knew, I was being taken into the delivery room. I was only in there ten minutes total. When I came to, I was laughing until you could hear me all over that ward. The doctor said that no one was going to believe me. He gave me a card that stated, "Frank Breech," with his name signed on it. God is faithful in all that he does. He once again gave me my life.

During the years of child bearing, I still had the valley

fever and was still affected by the sleeping sickness. My doctor told me that I was in worse physical condition than some eighty-year-old women and I was only eighteen.

Five years after Michael was born, I was sweeping the floor one day. I was talking to the Lord, as was my custom. I said, "Lord, what was that being that came into my room and told me of Michael's birth?" That still small voice said, "it was an angel of the Lord." I got goose bumps all over me. Why didn't I think of that? I pondered. At that moment I received that knowledge. Hum, my mother-in-law had tried to tell me that, but I wanted to know myself.

Debbie seemed to be doing just fine, even though they had said that neither of us would live. She grew even though she wasn't being fed regularly. I would lose consciousness for many hours, upon regaining consciousness it would take awhile to remember who I was, or where I was. Once I came to and her bottle warming on the stove had blown up all over the ceiling. We lived in the country, so no one knew that things were on this order. When Debbie was two years old, she had a fainting spell and turned blue. Her dad and grandma revived her with cold water. A few days later, she had another one of those fainting spells. We worked with her for a while before she revived. I took her to the doctor, and he didn't expect her to live through the night. He said that her blood count wasn't even half of what it should be. The next morning they gave her a blood transfusion. Her doctor said that she had pernicious anemia. God healed her. Our fourth child, Carl, was diagnosed with pernicious anemia when he was eight months old, and God healed him too.

We now had two wonderful children, and four more would arrive in the next few years. When our fourth child was born, Murvell asked me, "Are they all as exciting as the first? You act as if each one is your first baby all over again."

Yes, and I explained to her that each one is a new bundle of joy just as precious as the previous ones. Sherry arrived after Michael, Carl followed next, then Darrell, and Karen (Chanda) is the baby. None of the other deliveries were the same as Deborah and Michael's. Darrell's birth was very difficult because I had the Asiatic flu and he was five weeks early. Darrell was born with crippling rheumatic fever and was on crippled children's disability until God healed him when he was seven and a half years old. I will explain more about Darrell and his healing later.

Shortly after Sherry was born, we moved to Los Angeles and lived there for about two years. Carl had a new job there with better pay.

It was about four in the morning. Carl and I and the three babies pulled out of our driveway and headed for the big city. The sun wasn't up yet. I had many thoughts going through my head. Carl's brother and family lived in Los Angeles, and they were not in church. I pondered, will Carl get into this new place and join his brother and sister-in-law in other activities and will I be left at home to baby-sit our children, and theirs too, because of refusing to go to some of the places that they would go? With each turn of the wheels, I was being questioned in my spirit. What will you do? The Spirit of the Lord kept questioning me. As we reached the top of the Grapevine, I determined in my heart that regardless of what they all did, I would serve Jesus.

We had only been in LA a short while. It was once before payday, and any savings that we had were all gone. The cupboards were empty. The refrigerator only had metal racks shining through the lights. My father had gone to heaven, so I had no one to ask for a loan. Praise God, He is our source. I went to prayer. I repeatedly asked the Lord, "What am I going to feed my babies today?" The Lord repeatedly answered, "Get the eggs out of the refrigerator and feed them eggs." Each time I told the Lord, "There are no eggs in the refrigerator." Once again the Lord told me to go get the eggs out of the refrigerator. I said, "Come on, Lord, and I will show you that there are no eggs in the refrigerator." Arising from my place of prayer, I went into the kitchen and opened the refrigerator as I was saying, "Now see?" Wait! To my surprise there sat a dozen eggs. I know that Jesus miraculously placed those eggs there. There was no other way. I repented for doubt and disobedience. Each time I think of this, I repent that I would talk to my Lord in such a manner. He created all, He knows all. Why should I have contradicted His Word each time he spoke of the eggs in the refrigerator? In those days I spent four and five hours at a time in prayer, thinking that I had only spent about ten minutes each time. The Lord's presence and fellowship was so sweet during those times. Nothing could be compared to it.

# 5

During those months that we were in that place and I was having such sweet fellowship with the Lord, there were evil spirits and battles to be dealt with, too. In fact, the closer I got to God, the more Satan tried to battle me. One night I was sound asleep, and in my sleep, I am literally being pulled out of bed. I awake, open my eyes, and see this huge being that reaches from the ceiling to the floor. He is very broad and of the male gender. He is solid black. His blackness radiates a shine. He is holding his hands up in front of him with his palms turned toward me. The power in his hands are like those of a magnet. They are literally drawing me out of bed towards this awful creature.

I cried, "L-O-R-D!" Instantly the force or power that was holding me there released me. I fell immediately back on my pillow.

There was another incident that I will share in and through the blood of the Lord Jesus Christ, the lamb slain from the foundation of the world. The Lord was dealing with me about a deliverance ministry. I was thinking, *Okay, Lord, you are the one who does the work anyway.* The Lord revealed many things to me during that time. He allowed me to see angels, demons, imps, evil spirits of various types, etc. I disdain the appearance of these creatures, but I am able to cope because of the Lord. There is one exception, and I have repented before the Lord many times because of my cowardice at that time. I will try to tell about it in minute detail.

One Saturday night after I had spent much time in prayer, the Lord showed me a vision. He allowed me to see a horrible evil spirit that possessed an individual. It had to be dealt with and cast out of the man. I saw a creature with a body that was about two feet long. It was bright orange in color, with long shaggy hair. It had arms about a foot long, hanging all over its body. It had several tongues coming from its mouth. The tongues were about twelve inches long, and they were red/orange in color and continually wagging. This was such a horrible sight that I said, "Lord, please take this thing away." I said, "Jesus, I want to be close to you, but I don't want to be so close that I have all these demon powers to fight."

I am so sorry for saying that to our Lord and master. I have repented many times. It was only necessary to repent once. I want to be so close to Jesus. In fact, I want to be as close to Him as is humanly possible, regardless of all the enemies of hell, earth, or atmosphere. The Word says, "Greater is he that is in you, than he that is in the world" (I John 4:4) (KJV). In another passage, Jesus spoke and said, "I beheld Satan as lightning fall from heaven. Behold, I give unto you power to tread on serpents and scorpions, and over all the power of the enemy, and nothing shall by any means hurt you. Notwithstanding in this rejoice not, that the spirits are subject unto you; but rather rejoice, because your names are written in heaven" (Luke 10:18, 19, & 20) (KJV).

I did not know that this spirit would show up and be dealt with the very next night in the Sunday night service. There was a man whom we will call Edward (not the real name). He had missed church for two weeks. On this particular Sunday night when Edward's wife started to leave for church, he was lying on the sofa. She asked Edward if he wanted to go to church with her, even though he had not been himself lately. He made a gruesome noise and was literally thrown from the couch onto the floor. Edward managed to convey to his wife not to leave him behind, that indeed he wanted to go to church with her.

Upon arrival at church, she was unable to get him out of the car. She got the pastor to assist her. When Pastor Halyen went to the car to help, the evil spirit inside Edward threw him to the other side of the car. I was completely unaware of any of this until I looked up and coming down the aisle were Edward, his wife, and the pastor. At that moment I thought, *what in the world has happened to Edward? Has he had a stroke?* I pondered. *It seems as if he has some type of paralysis, or could he be drunk?* It was none of the above. He certainly did look awful, not at all like himself.

The pastor called everyone to the altar for prayer. He instructed that no one should be looking around. "Keep your head bowed, keep the blood of Jesus applied, and keep calling on the name of Jesus." All of the men gathered around and began to pray for Edward. The spirit acted violently. Pastor said, "Satan, what is your name?" With a growl it said in a husky voice, "Lust, my name is lust." They prayed for some time before deliverance came. It probably took thirty minutes or an hour. At one point it lifted eight big men off the floor, who were trying to restrain the violence of this spirit. All the while you could hear this spirit saying repeatedly, "I won't, I won't," to the commands of the pastor saying, "Come out of him." The church had double doors in the entry, they kept swinging wide open. The pastor sent someone to close them each time. After the doors swung open several times, the pastor sent someone to lock them.

There was an older woman watching the whole scenario in the spirit. Here is what she saw. She said when this spirit came out of Edward, she saw it. It was bright orange with long shaggy hair, arms all over its body, and many long tongues. The tongues were wagging continually and saying, "I won't, I won't." It went to a mother standing in the aisle, holding her baby, trying to keep it quiet as she prayed. The spirit went to the mouth of the mother and tried to enter. The older lady said, "I plead for the blood of Jesus over everyone in here, infants, mothers, everyone." At that moment it dropped to the floor, running to the back doors, screaming, "I won't, I won't."

The back doors flew open, the spirit ran out, the doors flew shut and locked. I didn't see the spirit with my eyes. I heard it every time it said, "I won't," in its refusal to leave Edward's vessel. I saw each time the door flew open. This never happened before or after that incident during the two years that I was there. I was amazed. There was a bar across the street from the church. I would not have wanted to be anyone in there that night. Spirits go seeking for someone to dwell in. I would not want to be anyone, anywhere without the blood of Jesus applied to my life.

Edward was a brand new man after that deliverance. The pastor instructed the entire congregation not to mention this to Edward. He was unaware of what happened to him. He had always been a cheerful, happy person to be around, seemingly in love with God and his wife. He grew cold in his walk with God. He began to criticize everything that was godly, including pastor's sermons. The door was open for evil to come in. This happened in a brief period of time. Praise God! He is faithful to help us if we truly want help. His mercies are new each morning, so the Word says. Blasphemy against the Holy Ghost is the only thing that we can never be forgiven for.

You now understand why I can only talk about this in

the name and through the blood of the Lamb. With the help of the Lord, I plan to obey, work, and please the Lord until He comes and catches us away.

The Lord gave me a vision, with a word of warning. While we were living in Los Angeles, the Lord gave me a vision of us being involved in a car wreck upon a ridge known as the Grapevine, the summit between Los Angeles and Bakersfield. He was instructing me as He gave the vision. He said, "Tell Carl and Earl (his brother) not to leave Los Angeles to go to Bakersfield on Friday night before the youth service at church." I told Carl and Earl what I had seen and heard. For about three months, they were faithful to obey these instructions. We would wait and go at another time. One weekend they had some business to take care of in Bakersfield that they were hoping to attend to on Friday evening before the establishments closed. They felt that they had waited long enough since the time that I received the warning. They decided that they would go.

I knew in my spirit that this was the time, so I determined not to go. Unbeknownst to me, Dorothy, Earl's wife, decided that she would not go. She too felt that this was the time that the wreck would happen. A short while before Carl was due to get home, the Lord spoke to me and said, "Get your babies and get in that car or they will all be killed," meaning everyone involved in the wreck. Hurriedly, I began to pack for the three little ones and myself. Carl was already packed, and I needed to be ready when he got home from work. I was expecting Carl, our fourth one, at that time.

I got into the car, knowing that I was on my way to a wreck. We were in Earl's car, and he was driving. We were now out of Los Angeles, climbing the Grapevine. I was looking down attending to Sherry, who was in my lap. Without looking up, I could see everything as it was happening. I looked up, and it was happening even as I had seen. There was a car stalled in front of us. This was in the days before the good freeway. We stopped without hitting the stalled car. Cars behind couldn't stop, so they would pull to the right to miss us and hit the car that was stalled. The stalled car was a bit sideways in both lanes, not leaving a clear lane for passing. The cars kept piling up with a crash. The right lane was full with no other place for them to go except to plow into the back of us.

I looked back and saw a big truck coming straight toward us at a rapid speed. There was no time to pray. I thought in my mind: *J-E-S-U-S!* Nothing happened, and nothing happened. I looked back and that big truck was backing up as fast as it had been coming toward us. I thought how could this be?

When traffic was restrained and people began to get out of their cars and exchange their parts of the incident, the driver of the big truck gave this report. He said, "I was coming up on this accident unable to stop, no way to turn, and the strangest thing happened. My truck somehow went into reverse. I do not know how it got into reverse. Suddenly I was backing down the highway as fast as I had been going forward!"

One of the newspapers that I read said, "Death fled the highway last night when fourteen cars piled up on the Grapevine."

The man responsible for causing the accident was drunk and his wife was pregnant. Drinking and driving, or drinking and living do not mix.

Carl, our fourth child, arrived several months after the wreck. He was unharmed. He was a very good baby and never cried for anything. I worked full time, so this was a blessing. We moved back to Bakersfield before Carl's first birthday. Before we made that move back to Bakersfield, I had a vision of moving to a place farther north than Bakersfield. In this vision we were living in the country in a gray farmhouse, but the house was a duplex. The kitchen doors opened into each other, and there was a very nice couple living in the other part of the duplex. They were a nice-looking couple. She had very short hair, and he had dark skin. God allowed me to know their names, which I will omit at this time. They had five children. God allowed me to see some personal things concerning this man and also concerning my husband about their personal walk with the Lord. That morning when my husband called me to breakfast, I said, "Wait, honey, until I pray first. I just had a dream about moving a way up north, and I've got to pray first."

My husband laughed at me. He said, "Oh, you dreamer, you." The next year on the anniversary date of that vision, we moved north to the place where the duplexes were. There was everything just like I had seen in the vision, even the very names of the people.

# 6

We spent the year before the move north in Bakersfield. That winter all of us had the Asiatic flu. There was a bad recession at that time. Thousands of people were laid off of their job, and my husband was one of those people. We were living on unemployment, and I was expecting our fifth child, Darrell. Financially, things were rough. I had to do laundry every day. Once the laundry did not get done for a few days. I was out of laundry detergent. I prayed and asked God to please give me some laundry detergent so I could have clean clothes for all of the family. In a few minutes, Debbie came in the house from play. She was carrying a giant box of Tide. "Here, Mom" she said. "The lady over the fence gave me this and told me to bring it to you." There was a fence on three sides, so I never knew which lady gave her the detergent.

I began to take in laundry and ironing in order to buy milk for the children. There was a lot of rain and fog, and I didn't have a dryer, so I had to pray for God to dry the clothes. Sometimes when it was raining or with fog all around, I would ask God to let there be sunshine and wind long enough to dry the laundry. God was so faithful to answer my prayers. He always did just that. Sometimes the sunshine and wind were in my yard only, or just over my clothesline. On a few occasions, I thought the children would enjoy seeing the sun and wind on our clothes while it was raining all around us, so I would invite them to come and look at how God answers prayers.

One night I was standing at the ironing board, trying to finish a lady's ironing so that I could have some money for milk for the children's breakfast. The Spirit of the Lord was all over me. The Lord was saying to me, "Your answer is at the door pressed down, shaken together, and running over so much so that you will not be able to contain it all." I was rejoicing and weeping before the Lord to the extent that my husband came, took me in his arms, and asked, "Do you need to go to the hospital? Are you in labor?"

"No, I am rejoicing in the Lord because the answer is on the way." At that moment there was a knock on the door; there stood a little elderly man and woman with a small box that had a half-gallon of milk and a loaf of bread in it. That looked wonderful to me. We thanked the couple and started to close the door. "Don't go away," they said, "there is more." A large truck backed up to our front porch and began to unload groceries. We knew none of these people. We were informed that the large markets, frozen food lockers, and produce establishments were giving groceries to many families who had been laid off of their employment. The blessing was so great that we could not contain it all. We received thirty-two loaves of bread, about that many half-gallons of milk; fresh meat, frozen meat, fresh produce, frozen produce, canned and fresh fruits and vegetables. There were crates of yams, cabbages, potatoes, apples, oranges, and bananas.

We filled the refrigerator and the cupboards; we put food in the closets, under the bed, and out in the garage. We took food up and down the street to the neighbors. We took groceries across town to others whom we knew were unemployed. My husband was embarrassed and grateful both at the same time while receiving this blessing. He has told me that he always got embarrassed when I told others how God would keep filling the meal barrel. Men are different. They feel that they are the providers, and rightly so. He now rejoices when he can share how God has always blessed us in various situations.

While we were in Bakersfield, before moving north to King City, Darrell was born. He was born five weeks early, and we moved when he was almost six weeks old.

I wanted one more little girl, and I asked God for her. Karen was born on Darrell's second birthday.

When I was pregnant with Karen, I experienced some difficulties. In the seventh month of my pregnancy, my face got a type of paralysis. My mouth puckered up into a peak. I looked awful and felt even worse than I looked. My memory was affected too.

I would be at the sink doing dishes, or some other type of housework, when I would feel the strangest sensation in my entire being. At first I was unaware of what was happening to me. I would always lose my memory of who and where I was. After a few times of this, I knew what to expect. Every time that strange sensation hit me, I knew what would follow. I would begin to rub my hands, face, arms, trying to hold onto consciousness. When I would come to, I would always be in my bed. My doctor said that this was nature's way of protecting me, but what about my babies? I had five of them running round unsupervised. I worried about the little ones. I was helpless to do anything about it.

When Deborah, our first child, was born, the doctors told me that one day I could forget everything. They said that there were two reasons: 1) the childhood injury that my female organs sustained could cause it and this was why they were recommending surgery at that young age; 2) the encephalitis (sleeping sickness). I was now pondering on this.

For a few years after Deborah was born, I would feel a strange feeling coming over me and I soon learned that I was about to fall into a deep sleep. When I would awake, I did not know where I was. I would see the surroundings in the room and remember that I had seen them somewhere before. It would take what seemed like hours before I could remember where I had seen those furnishings. I would remember where I was when I saw those furnishings and I would also remember who I was. When I knew that one of those sleeping attacks were coming on, I would run fast, get the babies, and put them in their cribs to try to protect them. I remember many times being outside hanging laundry. I would drop everything and run to get the babies in their cribs. I had not had one of those sleeping attacks for about three years.

Now there I was, almost four years later, in the seventh month of my last pregnancy and I was having what seemed to be the same kind of episodes. For a few weeks during that time, I couldn't seem to touch reality in its fullness. This brings a depression. Friends, family, people all around are laughing and having a wonderful time. I couldn't understand what was funny. I longed for the good old days when things were normal. I felt like someone who had fallen into the middle of the ocean with no arm long enough to reach them. It was scary. I had sense enough to know that if I had a cold or some disease, I could go and get a shot for the cure, but there was nothing for this. My doctor had told me that my uterus had turned completely upside down and was pressing on a nerve. He said that this was causing the problem, including the facial paralysis.

# 7

During this time I was running from the call to preach. I reasoned that no one was interested in hearing a female preacher. Every time I went somewhere to minister, someone would chide me and say women were not supposed to preach. Many times at church gatherings or while visiting family or friends, someone would invariably bring up the subject of women ministers with a negative tone so that I would be sure to get the message. At the ordination service where I was ordained, many ministers' wives came around and chided me for becoming ordained. They each told me that they could do all the preaching they wanted to because their husbands were ministers. My husband was a minister also, but I wasn't laboring on his calling. I didn't rebuke them. I had gotten the victory over this matter years before when I was running from the call.

Meanwhile, back to the scenario at hand. I would ask God to forgive me for shirking the call. I would minister for a while until I felt whipped again. I would start all over, telling my Heavenly Father that he must find someone else, that I just couldn't do it.

Karen's birth brought healing to mind and body. The times of loss of memory were over and so was the facial paralysis. A new problem had arisen, and at first I was not aware that there was a problem.

I hemorrhaged every day for several months after Karen's birth. At first I thought nothing of it; then I realized that something was wrong. I was afraid to go to the doctor. I was afraid of bad news. I put it off as long as I could, but I finally went to see the doctor. He ran a test and it came back positive. He said that I had cancer and I would need to have surgery. We were in revival at our church.

I went to the evangelist that Sunday morning and explained to him what the doctor had said. The evangelist asked me if I believed that God would heal me. "I sure do," I replied. The moment that he laid his hands on me, it felt as though I was struck by a bolt of lightning. Instantly the hemorrhaging stopped.

The church had a long sanctuary, and we were standing about halfway between the altar and the back door. The Spirit picked us both up, and it carried me to the back door and carried the evangelist to the front of the building, in front of the pulpit. The pastor's wife spoke with me afterwards. She said, "Sister Tiner, I wish that you could have seen it." She said that it looked as if a bolt of lightning hit us both, picked us up, and carried us. "The feet of neither of you touched the floor," she said. "You were carried to the back door, and he was carried to the front of the pulpit." That was almost forty years ago, and I am still healed. The week following the healing I went back to the doctor and the test came back negative; no cancer.

Shortly after being healed of cancer, I began once again telling Jesus that I cannot minister his gospel because some folks do not like women ministers. In a short while after telling Jesus that I could not minister, I had heart failure and spent a week in the hospital. While in the hospital, I won a young lady to the Lord. She had been in a car wreck that left her paralyzed from the neck down. Fourteen years later, in 1974, I read her testimony in the *Enquirer*. She said that her accident had caused her to find God and that God gave her courage for each day.

While I was in that hospital, God dealt with me about the call in my life. I would tell the Lord, "You will just have to take me this time, Jesus, I can't do it." I would think about my babies at home and my husband, and oh, how I wanted to see those babies. But I thought and thought, and I couldn't bring myself to promise God again that I would do it. I remembered the disdain folks had for female ministers.

One morning in the early hours, about two or three A.M., I began to say, "God if you will heal my body, I will preach your gospel." I asked to go home and since I was better, they let me go home. I preached for a little while and got the same chides as before. Once again I began to tell the Lord that I couldn't preach his gospel.

Not long after I once again decided that I couldn't preach because of peer pressure. I began having difficulty with my nerves. Everything made me jump out of my skin. I went to my doctor and told him of the extreme nervousness. He said that I must go away for a rest before I had a breakdown and had to be put away.

The enemy really tormented at that time. He would say, "You've really done it this time. God will never forgive you again. You have told him over and over that if He will heal your body that you will preach His Word. He will never answer you again. You will be lost forever." This always brought despair. It seemed as if my life was hanging by a thread. I kept the blood of Jesus applied to me at all times. I knew that as long as I stayed under the blood of the Lamb that the enemy could not touch me.

Esther, a friend, invited me to go with her to camp meeting at Santa Cruz. I accepted the offer, and what a wonderful ten days we had. My husband Carl and I had been married ten years. We took no vacations and kept our nose to the grindstone. We were both very hard workers.

The only reprieve that I got was when I was in the hospital sick or having a new baby. I enjoyed this time away for rest and spiritual renewal.

Camp meeting was awesome. We had a wonderful evangelist. I laughed, I worshiped the Lord, and I had fun. Ester and I would laugh and talk until sometimes four in the morning. The laughter and fun brought much healing to body and mind.

Esther had taken her camp trailer, and we went up to camp meeting on the night before camp started. She did this in order to get set up. I was so miserable that night and the next day because the enemy continued to torment me and accuse me. The Word of God tells us that the devil is an accuser of the brethren.

In the service that first night, the evangelist announced that sometime during the camp meeting he would call a healing line and pray for those who needed healing. In the beginning of that same service, the enemy perched on my left shoulder and continued to tell me, "You aren't going to be healed. You aren't even going to be forgiven for telling God that you cannot preach his Word. You will never be forgiven again." You cannot imagine the horrible feeling that came over me. I felt doomed. Jesus came at that moment and whispered in my right ear, "I will heal you tonight in this service; no one will lay their hands on you, you won't go through a prayer line. I will just come and heal you."

In a very short while after Jesus spoke those words to me, I felt the sweet presence of the Lord. I felt as though warm honey was being poured on my head and it was running all through my being and into my toes. At that very instant, I was healed. There was no more torment. I determined that I could preach the gospel, regardless of what the likes and dislikes of others were. Mankind is not

51

the one who asked me to preach the gospel. I must obey the one who called me at that young age of three. That was thirty-seven years ago, and since then I've never once told the Lord that I cannot preach His gospel. We must never try to please mankind above God and His plan for our lives.

On the very last night of that meeting, the evangelist asked for ten people to stand quickly to their feet and tell what God had done for them in that meeting. The Spirit was prompting me to stand and testify to my healing. I declined. I knew that out of three thousand plus people, ten people could stand before I had an opportunity. To my amazement nine people stood and no one else. I was holding onto the pew with both hands, determined not to stand. Lo and behold! Before I knew it, it was as if the Spirit of God had picked me up. I was in a cloud, sort of in a trance. I heard the evangelist say, "Someone get a microphone and get it to that little lady right back there."

I thought, *Oh, No! What kind of fair is this? No one else had to use a microphone.* Besides being heard in that large sanctuary it could be heard outside through the redwoods where thousands of other people were listening on the campgrounds. A gentleman came and held a microphone over my shoulder to me. I was so lost in the spirit that I do not know what I said.

The next day before we left camp, as I was walking on the grounds, hundreds of people would stop me to say, "You're that little lady who had such a wonderful testimony last night. You are the one who was running from the call of preaching. You were about to have a breakdown, and your doctor told you to go away and rest or be put away." Yes, that was me. I didn't know that I said all of that.

Life is so much more enjoyable now that I am healed. I can get out more and enjoy more things.

One Sunday morning we went out to get into the car to

go to church and there was no car. It had been stolen. The car was missing for three weeks before it was found. When we got it back, my husband told me, "I want you to lock this car regardless of how late you come home, even if you are alone." One night I went to a P.T.A. meeting. I took an uncle with me and left an aunt and uncle baby-sitting. Carl was working overtime as usual. When I came home from the P.T.A., there was a double trailer semi across the street loaded with tomatoes. Two men stepped out from behind the truck. I overheard one of them say, "There she is now; let's go get her." I said to my uncle, who was elderly and crippled, "Get in that house now." I heard one of those men say, "Oh, wait, she has a man with her." They stopped. The other man said, "I know him, I can handle him;" and they proceeded to cross the street.

I looked up and there stood an officer about seven foot tall. He had a sidearm on either side. I said, "Hi, boy, am I ever glad to see you!" That officer never returned my greeting. That was just fine with me, as long as he was there. I said to the officer, "Wait right there until I can get my car locked up." He did. He stopped and waited right there until I got the car locked. The two men hightailed it back across and down the street. The officer continued to follow those men. I stopped to watch. And I thought, *If he were a good officer, he would arrest those men.* He had to have heard what they said.

All of a sudden, while I was watching, there was no officer. It was dark, but the streetlights were on. Where did he go? Was there really an officer? One of my friends said to me after hearing about this incident, "Joy, you dumb-dumb you, that was no officer. That was your guardian angel." Be he angel or officer, he was sure in the right place at the right time.

Darrell is now three years old. Do you recall that earlier in the story I told you when he was twelve hours old they told me he was not going to make it? They took me to see him and half of his head was shaved. He had a large IV in one side of his head. His fever was very high. They informed me at that time that he had been born with an enlarged heart and crippling rheumatic fever. Later they informed me that he probably would not live past age three. However, should he live to be twenty or twenty-one, he would be just a vegetable in a wheel chair because of the high fevers, they informed me. During these three years of his life, he was having severe problems and continued to do so until God healed him at about seven and a half years of age. He had some type of fainting spells, and he would always turn purple with these spells. This was on a daily basis, sometimes three or four times a day. I would work to resuscitate him. He also got high fevers on a regular basis.

The fevers usually ran between one hundred four to one hundred six degrees. Once his temperature was a hundred and eight degrees. The doctor said they didn't usually live when it got that high. I often told folks that I had seven and a half years of nightmare with Darrell. I would wrap his head in a cold towel the minute I discovered a high temperature. I would always say, "Father, I apply this towel in Jesus' Name. I know that this towel cannot heal him, Father, but this is my works with my faith." This only added to the trauma of loss of memory when I told you that I was so concerned for my children in those days.

Darrell got a kidney infection. His body was swollen, and he had a rash. I was greatly concerned. He was in the hospital about forty-seven miles away. I went every day to see him, and I would spend a big part of the day with him. I had been telling God, "If you want him, there he is; just take him." I was trying to be submissive to the will of God.

God answered back. He said, "You say it with your lips, but you do not mean it with your heart."

I was sitting in church service one Sunday night having a battle in my spirit. I was thinking that I had served God all my life. Why would He not heal Darrell? *I think I will take my Bible and throw it in the nearest trash can.* I was so miserable with that decision. The congregation started singing, "I've Anchored in Jesus." Once again in my life, I determined in my heart, no matter what happens with Darrell, I am going to serve Jesus. Darrell came home from the hospital in a few days. Somewhere, underneath all the despair over Darrell's condition, I knew that God would heal him in His way and His time. I had always known this, even though I gave in to despair for a short time.

About a year after Darrell's bout with his kidney, Karen had a traumatic experience. She was now two years old. A heat wave went through King City. This was unusual. Karen got an influenza related to diphtheria due to that heat wave. The doctors said if she had been three instead of two, she could have fought it off better.

One afternoon Karen woke from a nap with difficulty breathing. My husband had just arrived home from work, and it was good that he did. He recognized the difficulty that Karen was having. I thought it was croup and that she would snap out of it. Carl said, "No! We've got to get her to the emergency now." He was right. She had to have a tracheotomy. That was an experience in itself. The trachea had to be suctioned periodically. It seemed as if she would choke to death when this procedure was performed. This was very scary.

In about a week, Karen was able to come home. This was not over; something worse was about to happen, and we were unaware of what was about to happen. Not even

55

the doctors could foresee the complication coming. We took our baby home, thinking that she would be okay. We had noticed that she seemed to be swelling in her body before we left the hospital, and we brought it to the doctor's attention. He didn't understand why she was doing this, but he thought that she would be all right. She mostly slept after going home. Each time that she awoke, she was bigger and more uncomfortable. We took her back to the hospital a couple of times. Each time they said that they did not know what was going on. They had us take her back home and told us to watch her.

This time when Karen awoke, she was about as broad as my two-hundred-pound husband. Her eyelids turned black and covered her eyes, and she couldn't see. Her eyes looked like two big balls on her face that was now dark. We hurried back to the emergency. Karen, in her dad's arms, said, "Daddy" over and over until her last breath was gone. A doctor and her daddy worked with her for an hour and a half by themselves, thinking that she was gone. They could find no pulse. Other doctors arrived to help. My husband would not let me be in there, so I am not sure what happened when they revived her.

Carl, my husband, said, "When he took her back to the hospital this final time, the doctor removed the tape that covered the place where the trachea had been." With their hands they began to move the air out of her body back through the opening of the trachea where it had entered. Air had gotten in through the opening and blown her skin up like a balloon. It collapsed one lung, and the other one was going fast. Praise God! They were able to get the air out and revive her. The doctors said that it would take at least three days for the lung to reinflate. To their amazement it inflated that same night before midnight. In another few days, she was able to come home from the hospital. Again I say, "Praise God!" I believe that it was a miracle that restored her life.

# 8

There seemed to be no good-paying jobs in the area. Carl worked overtime just to help make ends meet. I decided that we should move out of the area. We are both capable of earning good salaries. *We've done it before; we can do it again,* I thought. In my heart I knew that we were to be there to work with the youth. When I mentioned leaving to Carl, he said, "We can go, but we will be out of the will of the Lord. The Lord wants us here to work with the youth." "I know," I said, "but we have a family to support. In this small area, there just aren't jobs like we've had in the past." We decided to stay and trust God to meet our needs. The Lord spoke to me and said that he was going to take away my pride and humble me. That he would melt me like shortening. Melt me he did. It was ouch! all the way.

Families in the church bought clothes and shoes for the children and me. What an embarrassment! What a blessing! When the cupboards were bare, God would supply. One day the Lord told me that he was going to teach me not to despise the day of small things. I had no idea of what he meant, but before the day was over, I knew exactly what he was talking about. It was just before payday. I was in a quandary about what to do for dinner. There was nothing to fix. I started praying and inquiring of the Lord for the evening meal. The phone started ringing. Some church folks called and said, "Sister Tiner, can you use some potatoes for your evening meal? I seem to have cooked too many." On and on the phone rang, with someone offering me something that they had cooked too much of. Carolyn, a precious sister in the Lord, called and asked if I could use three corns on the cob already cooked. I said sure. My dad had taught us children if someone wants to give you something, do not refuse it or you would offend them. So I accepted the three ears of precooked corn. But I murmured to the Lord and said, "God, what am I going to do with three ears of corn? I have six children?" The Lord said to break them in half and give each of the children one. *Oh, yes,* I thought, *why did I not think of that?* We had twelve items of food that night all cooked and ready to go. That was thirty-seven years ago.

As I write this, I remember that it was twelve basketfuls of the little boy's lunch that Jesus had the disciples take up after feeding the multitude. Is there any significance? The Lord certainly taught me not to despise the day of small things. Something small in the Lord's hands becomes great. He took nothing and created the world. He hung the north over an empty space. God can do anything.

Once I had only one package of meat left in the freezer; it was a soup bone. Carl asked what was for lunch that morning before he left for the shop. He and the children all came home at noon. I cooked three hot meals a day. "Honey, I don't know. I've got one soup bone, and I'm going to put that on and start praying." The phone started ringing, with folks calling to see if I could use different produce items. When the family came home for lunch, I had a nice pot of soup that the Lord had prepared for them. Jesus never fails! He said that he wouldn't.

There is another occasion that I want to share with you, when God, our heavenly Father, put beef in the freezer. We were visiting some other ministers, we and some other folks. The subject came up that God owns all the cattle on the hills. The minister's wife, whom we were visiting, spoke up and said, "You just try and take one of those cattle and see how fast you go to jail." A light went on in my head. I thought to myself, *Yes, but if God reaches down and takes one of those cows off of the hill and gives it to you, no one will get into trouble.* At that moment in faith, believing, I asked my Heavenly Father for some beef for the freezer for the family. Three days later the farmer whom Carl had previously worked for called. "Could you use some beef for your freezer? We just had some butchered and it is too much for us. All you have to do is pay for the cutting and wrapping." Carl readily accepted. God keeps his promise; ask and ye shall receive. We lived in King City for almost five years and then moved back to Bakersfield.

I went to an oral surgeon and had a wisdom tooth cut out. He gave me some type of barbital. I believe that it was called, "sodium phenobarbital." The instant that I got the medication, I went out; at that same instant Jesus walked up beside me in a white robe. When I saw Jesus, I immediately pried my shoes off of my feet even though I was in a state of deep sleep. When the nurse started waking me up, Jesus started backing away until he was gone. I began asking, "Where is Jesus? He was here a minute ago." The nurse said, "I know, honey, but if you talk like that, you will scare your husband. He is coming to get you now." Later I was told that this was a truth serum and you could not tell a lie while under its influence. I asked myself, is this the reason why the nurse so readily agreed when I stated that Jesus had been there? Jesus proves himself time and again.

A couple of years after I saw Jesus at the dentist's office, he healed Darrell. Through the years before Darrell was healed, there would be those who would call and offer all types of support and prayer. Some even offered to pay for round-trip airline tickets for us to take Darrell to Oral

Roberts. I thanked them graciously and explained that God had not asked us to take Darrell to Oral Roberts or to anyone else. We have great confidence and respect for Oral Roberts. He has a lot of miracles, but man is not the healer, God is the healer. Man is the vessel that he sometimes work through. Should God have told us to take Darrell to Reverend Roberts or any other minister, we would have done so gladly. We told the good folk that God is everywhere and He can heal through our pastor or through any child of God who offers the prayer of faith.

One evening in 1965, a lady called. She said, "Sister Tiner, there is a faith healer in town. I believe that if you will take Darrell over to the meeting that God will heal him tonight." I said, "I think that I will just get ready and take Darrell." I hung up the phone to prepare the family to go to the service. The Lord spoke to me and said, "No! Don't take Darrell over there."

I hurried to my room, knelt beside my bed, and began to pray. I said, "Father, you have never told me what you plan to do about Darrell. I know that you are going to heal him someday in your way and your time, but you have never told when or where."

The Lord spoke. "I will heal Darrell shortly," He said. I jumped up excitedly and hurried to tell the family the good news. I called all of the family to me in the dining area of the house. I said, "I have some wonderful news!" By this time the enemy was planting seeds of doubt. It was as if I could see the word "IF" in big letters standing from the floor to the ceiling. I could hear a voice saying, *what if you only imagined that you heard the Lord say, "I will heal Darrell shortly"?*

I then said to the family, "Someday, IF God ever permits, I have a wonderful secret to tell you." Carl sent the children to bed early. Now what is the wonderful secret? I shared what the Lord told me. I shared also the big IF, and what if I had only imagined that the Lord had spoken those words to me. God's time called. "Shortly" appeared on the horizon soon because God did heal Darrell shortly.

This was in May 1965. Darrell had another bad virus. I always took my children to the doctor when they were sick. The doctor would usually run a test on Darrell after he was well to see if the virus had damaged his heart any more. The doctor ran more tests, and they all came back negative, nothing wrong. The doctor asked me if I could bring Darrell in another two weeks to be retested. He said that he wanted to have his equipment tested to be sure that it was working properly. In two weeks the new tests were run, and they too came back negative. The doctor then decided to call other heart specialists, including the main one out of Los Angeles. He asked if I could bring Darrell on August 12th to meet with them in the courtroom of the county hospital. I agreed to do so.

Ten heart specialists checked Darrell there in that courtroom of the hospital. They deliberated for a while. Then they told me, "Mrs. Tiner, we can't find anything wrong with Darrell's heart. We don't understand, but it is as if there has never been anything wrong with his heart. As of today we are taking him off of Crippled Children."

I took Darrell by the hand and started to the car. I was crying. I didn't know what we would do. Carl earned about $1,500 a month if the oil rigs were not down and he was working. That was good pay for those years, but if weather or something prevented him from working, we had to have a cushion to see us through.

Insurance paid 80 percent of Darrell's medical bills. That twenty percent could get spent if he had to be hospitalized often. I murmured to God, "God, what are we going to do if Darrell needs to be hospitalized again?"

"Did not I tell you that I would heal Darrell shortly?" was his reply. "Oh, yes! You did." I was then troubled no more about the matter. It was a good healing. Darrell is now forty-two and has never had another problem with his heart or his joints.

Darrell never became a vegetable, as was predicted. My aunt once said to me after baby-sitting for the evening, "Joy, if this boy is as smart at nineteen years as he is at nineteen months, I do not know what you will do with him." I thought, *Sure, sure, Aunt Sue, you are just provoked at him.* However, when Darrell was in the first grade, his teacher called me in and said, "Mrs. Tiner, your son is six years old and has the mind of a sixteen-year-old. It could get him into trouble," she said.

When he was seven years old, his heart specialist evaluated him and checked his I.Q. He called me in and said, "Mrs. Tiner, I don't know if you are aware of it or not, but your child has a very high I.Q. This is the kind that should go on and be a scientist or an engineer. These are the kind that usually drop out at about twelve years of age because there is nothing to challenge them," he informed me.

When Darrell was in the fifth grade, his teacher called me in to discuss his I.Q. She said, "Mrs. Tiner, we have no way to test how high Darrell's I.Q. is." She showed me some cards for testing and said, "This is superior senior material and he is above, way above superior." It ran off the top of the material.

When Darrell has gone to academies, his test score has always been higher than some with four- and eight-year degrees. His doctor was right; he started trying to drop out of school when he was twelve and again when he was in the eighth grade.

The intent here is not to say how smart or intelligent Darrell is. But rather to say how faithful God is to turn about a situation that could be so negative and so bleak to an individual or an entire household.

It was during this same time when I was told that I wasn't expected to live long enough to raise my children. I applied for employment where they train you for a specific job. I had to take a test to see if I qualified. I did qualify. When I inquired about the test results and when could I start training, I was informed, "we have checked your medical records and they do not expect you to live long enough to raise your children. Therefore you cannot be trained." I was disappointed. I was not expecting to die. My medical doctors had always told me never take a job and go to work, not even when my children were grown when I thought that I could. Little did they know I worked every chance I got. From candling eggs to driving the school bus.

I know that no one is assured of that next breath or next moment in time. valley fever began to be active in a big way. I would almost collapse walking from the bed to the bath. Sometimes it seemed as if that next breath wasn't there. Our church was having revival. I tried to be faithful and be there. One night I was so miserable and I couldn't get warm, so I wore my high-heel snow boots and took a shawl to throw over my lap. It was wintry and cold outside.

I was sitting near the front on the second pew. The Lord began to tell me that if I would run to the back door and back three times that he would heal me. I said, "Lord, I am always the one who makes a spectacle. Besides that, Lord, I have on these high-heel snow boots and there is no carpet on this floor. The noise would be too great. I can't do it, Lord."

The Lord said, "If you don't do it, you will die." "Lord, I just can't do it."

About that time the evangelist stopped preaching. He looked right at me and said, "One time we were in a revival.

There was an elderly gentleman sitting about were Sister Tiner is sitting. He had an incurable disease. The Lord told him that if he would run to the back door and back three times that he would heal him. He refused to do so and he died."

I thought, *My goodness, how can he know what God said to me?* I jumped up, running down the aisle shouting and praising God as I went. The Lord spoke into my ear and said, "Because you didn't obey when I first told you, you must run outside through the side door three times." I obeyed this time. I have never been bothered with valley fever since that time, and that was thirty-five years ago.

Let me share something about that side door with you. I did not know that the only way to open that door was to press down on a bar inside the building. I did not realize that the knob on the outside was a permanent fixture that could not turn. I ran out the back door around to the side door. When I grabbed that knob, it literally turned in my hand before I could try to turn it. I thought, *How strange, maybe someone is on the inside turning it.* I did this three times as I was told, and I received my healing. When the sermon was over, the pastor took the pulpit. He said, "Sister Tiner, I want to know, how did you get that door opened?" Before I could reply, he stated that the only way to open that door was with the bar on the inside.

He rolled the waters of Jordan and the Red Sea. Is there anything that you think He cannot do?

# 9

In another few years, Carl and I would have to decide if we were going to stay in the ministry, go full time, or get out altogether. The heavenly Father had been dealing with Carl about that. The Lord told Carl that it was time to pull up roots, give up the job, get rid of the house, and go full time in the ministry. Carl said, "God, if this is you talking to me, please tell Joy. God, you know how women like security." God did begin to tell me verbatim as he had told Carl.

I went to Carl and began to share with him the things that God had told me. He said, "God has been speaking to me too. I asked him to please put it in your heart too because I know how you love security." Carl resigned from his job in environmental health and also from the church where we were pastoring.

We had been fasting and praying about where the Lord wanted us to go. The Lord woke me up one night and gave me a vision, saying, "Go to Arizona." When I came out of the vision, I sat straight up in bed, crossed my arms, and asked, "Why God? What did we ever do to deserve Arizona?" I was foolish and ignorant in more ways than one. I thought Arizona was just a desert. I knew nothing about Arizona or of its beauties, its advantages, or anything. My first thought was not to tell Carl what God had shown me. *If he chooses the wrong place, that will be him and not me,* I reasoned. I did tell Carl, and I was glad that I did. God gave him a vision, told him Arizona, and let him see the snow.

Carl said he thought this vision might not be God, "I don't think it snows in Arizona." We were both ignorant about Arizona.

My most foolish behavior was to question God like that. Whoever heard of the clay arguing with the potter? I've repented, and I am thankful that God never wiped me out. I am ashamed of that behavior, and I praise God that His mercies are new each morning.

We sold most of our furnishings and went to a small town east of Phoenix. We were there for two years when the Lord called us to evangelize for a time. Arizona was one of the highlights of our life. The people were wonderful and God blessed us in so many ways. Our son Michael encountered quite an experience while we were there.

One evening Michael came to me and said, "Mom, ever since you brought me home from the hospital when you wrapped me in a blanket and took me to church, you've been taking me ever since. I want to see what the other side of life is about." He found out that very night. It was women's night at the "Y," so I went with the ladies. I felt a strange uneasiness and told the ladies that I was going home. When I got home, I asked, "Where is Michael?" His dad said he had walked downtown for a while. The uneasiness grew. I stayed in prayer throughout the evening. The family went to bed around eleven P.M., but no one could sleep. That is everyone except for Darrell. He pulled up a chair by the front door and said, "I'm going to be sitting right here when Michael comes through the door. I saw him and his friend get into a car with some strangers this evening downtown."

Sherry went to Michael's room and got into his bed so that she would be sure to wake up when he got home. The Lord prompted me to get out of bed and urgently pray. I felt impressed in the spirit to demand Michael to get up and get home. I said, "Michael, get up! Get up wherever you are. Get up, and get home in the name of Jesus!"

Michael crawled through his bedroom window about two-thirty in the morning. He was a bloody mess. What was left of his shirt was nothing but blood, and his nose was black and swollen over his face. In fact his face was bruised and swollen. Dad cleaned him up and took him to the emergency room where they found him to have a broken nose and to be badly bruised.

Michael said when he and his friend went downtown that evening, they saw these three men coming out of a tavern. They approached the men and asked, "Will you buy us some alcohol? We have money and will pay for yours, too. We are too young and they will not sell it to us." Michael was seventeen, and his friend was fifteen.

The men agreed and bought the alcohol. That was when Darrell saw them get into the car with the strangers. The young friend got sick from the alcohol in a hurry and the strange men did not want this kid throwing up on them or in the car, so they dropped him off somewhere. They took Michael twelve miles out of town on the river and planned to kill him. They were fighting him and trying to get him to fight them one at a time to see which one was a better fighter. Michael told them no, that he did not want to fight. They pushed Mike to the ground, and while he was on all fours, the largest of the men, weighing about two hundred thirty pounds, sat on him while the other two kicked him in the face, ribs, and body.

Michael said they had almost got him flat on the ground at one point, and he knew if they did that, he would never get up. At that moment he said a strange thing happened. He heard my voice saying, "Michael, get up! Get up wherever you are! Get up and get home in the name of Jesus." A superhuman strength came over him, and he threw the man off of him and took off running down the riverbed where the car could not go. He said that they followed the riverbed quite a while, shining the car lights trying to locate him. He said that he had to dodge several dogs, some places having two big German shepherds.

I have made many failures in my walk with the Lord. The one that grieves me the most happened while we were still pastoring in a small town. We were preparing to go away for a few days. Our first grandchild was about to be born, and that was back in California. I wanted to be there for that blessed event. The Lord had been trying to get my attention all day, but I was too busy. I was hurriedly trying to prepare to leave that evening.

There was a young man whom I will call Timmy Hanks (not his real name). The Lord repeatedly said to me that day, "You need to pray for Timmy Hanks or he will be killed." I said, "Lord, I don't even know a Timmy Hanks." The Lord said, "Yes, you do. You met him and his family two weeks ago at the church eight miles up the road." So then I remembered who Timmy Hanks was. The rest of the day I ran through the house, packing and whispering a prayer as I went. I was saying, "Father, please protect Timmy Hanks." I had never once stopped and interceded in prayer for him. I was so ashamed that I failed in that respect.

Later that night, before we left for California, the Lord spoke in my ear and said, "In a few days, when you get home, a woman will call you and tell you that Timmy Hanks is dead." In a few days when I got home, the phone rang and the woman's voice on the other end of the line said, "Did you hear that Timmy Hanks is dead?" "No! What happened?" I asked. "He was a construction worker and was on top of a new building that was being constructed when he fell off, landing on a metal stub below." I weep and repent every time I think about how I failed the Lord, Timmy Hanks, and his family. There is a power in prayer. The Bible says to pray without ceasing.

There is one more incident that occurred before we left town that I want to share with you. There was a lady in the church whom I will call, "Sister Brown." That is not her real name. She came a few times and discussed her husband and his mistress with me. I would always pray with her. She shared with me how she feared for her life and how this other lady was continually doing things to endanger her life.

One morning Sister Brown came to the parsonage, "Sister Tiner, we've got to pray. Last night when I went home from church, that lady was parked across the street from my house. When I started to go into my house, she fired a gun at me. The bullet grazed through my hair, just missing my head." I said, "Sister Brown, the Lord is tired of this. He is not going to put up with this any longer. Your husband must repent and tell the other woman to get lost, or he will find himself in hell or disabled. If your husband does not repent, God will allow his life to be taken. God may give him a deathbed repentance if he changes his ways. God is a merciful God."

I was unaware that Sister Brown was angry with me over this prophecy. We left the state shortly after that, and I didn't see Sister Brown again for three years. Three years later we went back to visit. Sister Brown and her husband were there in church. Her husband had partial paralysis from a stroke. They both graciously received me with a warm welcome. She said, "Sister Tiner, when you left here, I was very angry with you. I stood up one Sunday morning and told the entire congregation what you said about my husband. I want you to know that I am so sorry for that. Everything happened just like you said it would. My husband had a deathbed repentance because God was merciful. His kidneys had already failed, and the doctor said there was no way that he was going to make it. When he repented, things changed. Today he sits here a changed man, serving God." They thanked me for being obedient to the spirit of God. I in myself had no way of knowing that would happen to that man. Only after the Spirit of God breathed on me was I able to know that.

A couple of months before I prophesied to Sister Brown about what was about to happen, I was in making up my bed when the Lord began to tell me of some places that he was taking us. He had previously told Carl and me that he wanted us to resign and go into evangelistic work. Today he laid out the whole itinerary that we were to take. He had told us to go into Washington State. Some of the names of the places that we were to go were so funny. I had an excuse for every one of them. I thought, *This can't be you, Lord.* I thought that funny names were running through my head when I heard the name of one town such as Kellogg. I stopped spreading covers on the bed and went to look to see if the cereal had been left out, but no cereal had been left out.

When he said, "Pasco," I said, "There is a service station by that name." He spoke "Walla Walla." "I recognize that name, Lord. I was there once." He spoke the name "Wallace." "I have a relative by that name." He spoke "Marshall." "I had a principal with that name." He spoke the name "Dayton." "And there is a brand of tires by that name." He spoke the name "Starbuck."

"Oh, how funny. Who ever heard of such a name?" When I got the atlas there was every name that he had mentioned to me.

Before we leave this small town in Arizona and go to

Washington State for revivals, I want to share another incident that happened that summer.

We had two very young couples who were evangelists who came for a revival. We had seventy to a hundred young people in the church. Therefore a young evangelist would be good for the youth. It was a Saturday morning, Carl and I were out doing visitations. We were going to go shopping as soon as we were through with visitations. we were at the house of the last parishioner on the list.

The Lord spoke to me and said, "Go home now, do not go shopping. Go home now." I whispered to Carl and said, "Honey, we have got to go home now." We graciously excused ourselves and left.

Once in the car, I said, "Honey, we can't go shopping. We need to go home now." "Why?" he asked.

"I don't know why. The Lord said to go home." When we got home, I felt impelled to go into the church to pray. While kneeling at the altar, I had a revelation. I could see some of the children under a train in the canyon down below our house. I started to get up and scream at the same time. I had got up on one knee and I was about to say Carl, "We have got to get to the train now." There was big hand on my shoulder that pushed me back down, and a voice that said, "Get to that altar and pray. There is no time to go to the train." We prayed for some time until we felt peace and victory over the situation.

Later when we got into the car, to go shopping, Karen was hiding in the back seat because she wanted to go with us. Carl said, "Honey, why did we need to rush home from visitation; and why did we need to go into the church to pray?" "I don't know," I said.

"Did the Lord show you anything?" he asked. "No, some silly picture ran through my head. I could see some of the kids under the train. The train was taking off with them under there."

Karen popped up from the back seat. She said, "Mother, that was no silly picture; that really happened. I promised that I would never tell. The kids don't want to get into trouble, so they don't want you to know. But here is what happened. You know how the train sits on those tracks and never moves. We waited and waited; finally we decided to wait no longer. All of us had gotten across the tracks, except Sherry and Lori's dog. The train took off with Sherry under there. The dog ran out. We do not know or understand how Sherry got out without being killed or cut up." Once again God is faithful.

The thing that was so tempting and enticing on the other side of the tracks was a river with a swimming hole. There was a big tire swing, swung on a long rope from high up in a tree. Young people enjoyed going there to play. The four young evangelists, our six children, and the church and neighborhood youth were the ones who crossed under the train that day. For six months that year, our six children were teens at the same time. Karen was thirteen and Deborah was nineteen. That was one of the happiest times of our life. The children were always playing tricks on each other. It was humorous and enjoyable.

When we left Arizona, we wanted to go through Bakersfield to say hello and good-bye to our families. We sold everything once again, and we bought a new twenty-eight-foot motor home to travel in while we were evangelizing. We didn't want to be a burden to anyone, and we needed some type of security for the family. We were left with a small savings to keep us until the Lord provided more. We were going by faith because no churches had been contacted. We were being obedient to the call. I was a bit concerned about this. It cost ninety-five dollars every time we filled that big tank; it was a ninety-five gallon tank. I wondered if we should take the money out of our budget to go through Bakersfield.

In Bakersfield there was a pastor who asked if we would come and minister that Sunday morning. It was a small church, and so they couldn't afford to give us an offering for our ministry. I was concerned about this too, since time and money were limited. The Lord spoke to me and said, "If you will be faithful to and go to this congregation, when you get back in town, a little old man will come up to your motor home and give you a hundred dollars." That happened just like the Lord said. I was surprised when I saw who the little old man was.

Another church in a town north of Bakersfield contacted us and asked if we would come for a revival. They said that they were small and it was difficult to get an evangelist who would go to out-of-the-way places. We felt impressed to go, not knowing if there would be any kind of support. The revival was great. The Lord and the people blessed us mightily. You never waste time if you are doing the Lord's will.

Those were the days of inflation. You would wait quite a while in a line to get gas for your vehicle, and we were en route to Washington State. We had been traveling for hours, but we found no place open for gas. We traveled all night, knowing that our vehicle would travel ten hours on one tank of gas. We traveled through the mountains for some time, until the gas tank read empty. In the curves there was no place to pull over. We kept traveling and praying. It was just becoming daylight. Carl spied an area up ahead, on the other side of the highway that looked large enough to park the motor home. He coasted into that spot just as the engine sputtered its last sputter. He and Darrell got out and got the gas can. Darrell hitched a ride into town. Someone at the station brought him back to the motor home. Our God is merciful and faithful.

# 10

The night of our first service in Washington, when Carl got up to minister, he said, "Folks, we want to thank God for a safe landing in Washington." Karen and I bit our lips to prevent us from hilarious laughter. The truth of the matter was that Carl did have a safe landing that very first night. Karen had forgotten the water dish for Babe, her whippet hound, and left it on the step just inside the motor home. Carl got all spiffed up in his new suit, shirt, and tie, with not a hair out of place, perfect to the T. He looked so debonair. He started down the steps, opened the door, and slid right out onto the ground on his backside! Dust and dirt were flying. Karen froze. She knew that she was in trouble then. Carl got up and brushed himself off as he was saying, "K-a-r-e-n! How many times have I asked you to put that drinking dish away when Babe is through with it?" He got all cleaned up again and tried it once more. Once he was outside, we could hold it no longer. We roared with laughter.

All the meetings were exceptional. The heavenly Father ministered to so many needs. At one place where we went for revival, there was an elderly gentleman who came into the prayer line one night. He was eighty years old. One lung had not functioned for fifteen years due to the mine work that he had done; the doctors had told him that there was nothing that could be done. He asked for healing for that lung. The next night he came and went back through the healing line again. I thought that he liked the feeling of the presence of the Lord that he had felt the night before and decided to come for another touch of the Lord.

Carl said, "What would you like tonight, sir?" With tears running down his face, he said, "I want to be saved." Right there in that prayer line, he said the sinner's prayer. He then told the congregation that he had gone back to the doctor that day. The doctor asked him, "What had happened to you? That lung of yours that has not worked for fifteen years is now working." We serve a wonderful Creator.

The Lord allowed us to minister in a number of places. We saw the Lord heal cancer, heart disease, kidney failure, and numerous other conditions. We always told folks to keep taking their medicine. If you are truly healed, it will show. Some have contacted us later to testify to the fact that the doctor said that they no longer needed their medication.

At one of the places where we went for revival, a young lady came forward for healing for her eye. She said that she had no iris or pupil in that one eye and that she could not see out of it. We looked at her eye and we could see nothing but white. She asked if God would heal her. She was a college student. It seemed that healing was something that she knew little about. She was attractive. We prayed for her, and immediately there was a brown speck that came in. Carl said to me, "I've got to pray for others. You stay here with her and keep praying." Soon she had a brown iris with a pupil in it. She covered her good eye, and looking back at the clock on the back wall, she could tell time with the newly healed eye.

After a time we began pastoring again. The Lord continued to show himself mighty and wonderful.

Twice in my life, the Lord allowed me to look into outer darkness. I will share the first time with you now. If the Lord permits, I will share the second time with you later.

One morning in February or March of 1978, at two-thirty in the morning the Lord woke me up and said, "I want to let you look into outer darkness, and look at lost spirits in hell."

I will explain it as best I can. If you were to look down into a deep canyon and see the canyon floor and see a lake or river running through that floor and see little cabins or abodes on that canyon floor on the bank of that lake, that is what outer darkness looks like. If you took a mirror out and let the sun shine on it, it would be so bright that you could not look at it. The floor of outer darkness reflects back at you such as the mirror does. The only difference is the reflection in darkness that reflects at you with a horrible, eerie sensation.

The abodes there weren't much bigger than the old-fashioned outhouses. I recognized some of the people there. I had known them in this life. They had their dwelling and abode there, and they were very mean. I had only been in that place a short while when suddenly I had the urge to bury my face in my hands and wail and gnash my teeth. I could not have borne it except somehow I thought the Lord was close by watching over me, although I could not see him or feel his presence. I remembered that he said that he was going to let me go there and look.

At the time when I felt like weeping, wailing, and gnashing my teeth, Satan showed up. He said, "Most people, by the time that they reach this point, begin to wail and gnash their teeth." He was trying to harass me into doing the same.

The scene changed. The Lord allowed me to look and see the lost souls in hell. Who do you think is the most miserable person in hell? It is that backslidden preacher. The second most miserable persons were the actors and actresses who didn't make heaven.

There was a preacher there whom I had known on earth. He repeatedly preached a salvation message. At the close of each message, he would give an altar call. He would say, "if you will only come to this old-fashioned altar and invite Jesus into your heart and ask Him to wash you with His blood, you can be saved." Every soul in there would always stop whatever it was that they were doing and bow at that altar and invite Jesus in. This act was repeated over and over, all to no avail.

Everyone in that place continued on with the things that they were doing on earth. The actors and the actresses continued on with their acting. They would no sooner get through with one drama than they had to start another one. Oh, how they hated that. They longed to be free from it, but there was no way; this was their doom for all eternity. The only time that anyone got any reprieve from the things that they were bound to was when the minister gave the altar call and they stopped everything to bow their knee at the altar. Jesus brought me out of outer darkness, and I was glad to be back in my room.

I do not pretend to know the mystery of hell and outer darkness. I know that the Bible, the Word of God, says: "And death and hell were cast into the lake of fire." This is the second death. "And whosoever was not found written in the book of life was cast into the lake of fire" (Revelation 20:14 & 15). (KJV)

Are you aware that the children of God are the salt of the earth spiritually speaking? (Matthew 5:13). "Ye are the salt of the earth: but if the salt have lost his savor, wherewith shall it be salted? It is thenceforth good for nothing, but to be cast out, and to be trodden under foot of men" (KJV).

Salt is a preserving agent. Let us be so salty in the Lord that we never lose our savor, but be that preserving agent wherever the Lord intends. Let me give you an example. We were traveling over the Snoqualmie Pass one evening in May. A freak snowstorm came up. We weren't prepared to travel on ice and were having great difficulty. A small white car with chains sped around us at an unsafe rate of speed. Up the road aways, it got into a slide and started over the embankment on the opposite side of the highway. I said, "Father, in the name of Jesus, stop that car." The car stopped instantly. Sherry said, "Mother, they don't know that there are Christians back here praying." They too may have been Christians. I believe that God used us as salt at that moment.

God promises in his word that if we will be faithful to serve him, he will save our household if they believe in him. My twin was always confused about religion. The Lord woke me up in the early hours and gave me a vision about him. The Lord said, "I'm going to take him. Deathbed repentance is the only way for him to be saved. It will be not quite two years." Twenty-two months later, my twin went to be with the Lord on deathbed repentance. God is merciful and faithful, and no one should put it off, thinking that they will have a chance prior to exiting this life. We know of instances where the young have been snuffed out without a hope of repentance. The last such incident that we knew about was of the young man coming to the Lord a few days before his accident.

May we be so salty in the Lord that others will want to drink of the living waters. May our lives help show the way to the straight and narrow path that leads to that celestial city where the streets are paved with gold, and where the Lamb is the light of that city. Let us labor that none be cast into outer darkness where there is weeping and gnashing of teeth.

In October of 1986, the Lord woke me in the early morning hours and permitted me to look again into outer darkness.

In one of the churches where we pastored, we had a deacon whom I will call Brother White (not his real name). He seemingly was a very nice person. He supported the gospel well and seemed to be a good man. There were some things that happened in the church. Things that others were involved in that neither we nor anyone else had any control over. The happenings weren't serious, only minor things. Brother White got angry with the pastor and quit the church. He avoided the pastor, saying that he could never forgive this.

Carl and I decided that we should resign so that this man would return to the house of God. Brother White had cancer, and we wanted him to have the support of the church. We were young, so I am not sure that we should have resigned for that reason. Brother White did return back to the fellowship when we resigned. He passed away a few months after we left.

On this morning in 1986, the Lord permitted me to go to a place that looked like outer darkness. I was taken into a place that looked like a prison house. There was no light; everything was seen in the dimness. There was a large being in the reception area, acting as keeper of the prison house. When I arrived he immediately gave some keys to another smaller-type being with the instruction, "Bring Mr. White in." The being did as it was told. It went and unlocked a place that looked like a jail cell and brought Mr. White into the reception area.

When Brother White came in, I greeted him as I did

when he was on earth. I said, "Good morning, Brother White, how are you today?" He greeted me graciously and said, "Not doing so good today, just about like yesterday. Like on earth, some days are better than others. While a person is breathing in life is the time to prepare for eternity. Find my granddaughter Martha (not her real name) and tell her that in life is the time to prepare. I do not want her to come here." The visit then ended, and he was being taken back to his cell.

It would appear that a lost soul in eternity is never healed of this disease. Do you recall my other visit to outer darkness when I saw lost souls in hell? I saw them bound forever to whatever they were doing on earth. I suppose that sickness and disease are the same for those who go to that abode.

We must always forgive everyone no matter what wrong he or she has done us. Even if we only think that they have wronged us, we must forgive them. Jesus said, "If we do not forgive others, neither will our heavenly Father forgive us."

We moved South again. We were living in a place where the water had gotten contaminated. When we moved there, the Lord instructed me to buy drinking water. I thought that I would be selfish if I did so, and I did not obey. I got sick unto death. I couldn't eat and I lost weight. I got sicker and sicker. The doctors couldn't find what was wrong. Some of our friends invited us for dinner. A friend said, "Joy, I know that you can't eat, but I will make you some Jell-O." I considered not keeping that engagement. I thought, *I'm going to die soon and I'm just too sick to go. Carl can go and I'll just stay in bed.*

The Lord spoke to me and said, "If you're just going to die anyway, why don't you go? You can be miserable there the same as here and you won't be alone."

When we entered the house of our friends, the gentleman looked at me and said, "Sister Tiner, you look gangrenous." I thought, *I know, but do you have to say that?* I'm miserable enough without being reminded from someone else. Now I am thankful that he did say that. I think it played a part in my healing. We were sitting around fellowshipping and talking about the Lord after they had anointed and prayed for me. Throughout the evening the spirit of the Lord hit me about four times. Every time I felt the spirit, I jumped up and did a Holy Ghost dance. Before I left there that night, I knew that something supernatural had happened. I could now get well. The thing that had me sick unto death was now taken care of by our loving heavenly Father. With medication and time, I could now heal naturally.

About a year after this bout with sickness, I went to take care of my mother. I took care of Mama for eight years before the Lord called her home. I still miss my mother. I know that I will see her in heaven.

The year that the Lord called my mother, the Lord showed me five months prior to her death that she was making a change. I won't go into detail here to explain what the Lord showed me about Mama, but it was beautiful. A short time after the Lord showed me that she was making a change, the Lord came to visit her. I don't know if she recognized Him as the Lord.

I went to a women's ministry fellowship. We started at ten in the morning and had service and potluck until about two in the afternoon. When I arrived home, Carl said, "Go into your mom's room. She wants to tell you something." I entered the room, and Mom said, "Joy, I've got something to tell you." "What is it?" I asked. "Today a man came into my room and said, 'Set your house in order, for I am coming for you soon.' "

I knew immediately that it was the Lord speaking to her. Nevertheless, I said, "Are you sure, Mom? You probably just had a dream."

"No! I didn't," was her instant reply. "I know what I'm talking about" she continued. "He was in here." I knew but I wanted to be sure.

Carl and I discussed this later. Mom had called Carl to her and told Him of the incident while I was at the women's meeting. He too told her that it was probably a dream. She, however, was as emphatic with Carl as she was with me. She then began asking everyone who came to visit to pray the sinner's prayer with her for her salvation. Four months later Mom went to be with the Lord. I still grieve over her. However, I know someday I will be with her again.

At this present moment, I do not know ABBA FATHER'S next assignment. Be it life, death, or rapture, I want to please him in it.

Children, I have written about many personal things. Things that could be embarrassing. I want you to know the real God who moves and breathes on real-life situations. I am not expecting to die, but should Jesus call me away to be with him, I want you and others to know that there is a God who created all things. He still works in mysterious ways. His ways are higher than our ways; even as high as the heavens are above the earth.

So please, children, be prepared and ready at all times should Jesus call you to come and live with him, with me, with others in our heavenly home.

I have shared many wonderful and strange experiences with you children. Most of these experiences have had a good or joyous ending, with the exception of the man whom God asked me to pray for or he would be killed. I sometimes hesitate to share some of the things that God shows me because some might think it silly. Nevertheless, I would rather please God than man. Let me share just such an experience.

Carl and I were traveling. We were going to visit one of our daughters and her family. We stopped for gas, and across the street was a dance studio. A teacher and her student could be seen through large picture windows. The student looked to be about eight to ten years old. They were doing ballet. Suddenly I had the strongest urge that they should lock up and get out of there. I felt like running across the street and telling the teacher that she needed to leave or she would be murdered. My pride didn't let me go tell her. I thought that she would think that I was silly. The next morning I read in the paper that she had been knifed and killed. I have wondered many times had I gone and warned her, would she have listened or would she have laughed at me? God knows all things and He wants all of his creation to hear and know when He speaks. God is not a respecter of persons. He wants to speak to everyone.

There is another experience of a different type that I want to share. Carl and I, and some other members of the family, were in Texas for a revival many years ago. There was a terrible heat wave. The heat wave was so severe that some committed suicide. The Lord showed me a vision on our way home to Washington state, stalled in a desert with the car overheated. The Lord told me to tell Carl to get new hoses to carry back with us. I told Carl what I had seen and what the Lord had said. Carl informed me that the hoses on the car were new and that they were all right.

Nevertheless, at my request, he looked under the hood. Everything was fine. When we got home, we went to visit one of our daughters about an hour away in Oregon. We left that evening to go back to our house. The Lord told me that we were to go back to our daughter's or someone would be killed; it seemed as if it would be our daughter

85

and son-in-law. We turned around, went back, and spent the night with the kids.

The next morning we started home again. We had only gone a short distance when our car heated up. We pulled off the highway down by the river. Our hose was busted, so we were stranded, but not for long. We looked and saw a car coming from town in the direction from which we ourselves had just come. The car pulled down to where we were. A gentleman got out and handed Carl a container for dipping water and a roll of tape. He said, "Here, you need this." He got into his car, turned around, and went back into town. Carl and I believe that this was probably an angel. God is so faithful. The Word says, "Be mindful to entertain strangers, for in doing so some have entertained angels unawares." You must be discerning of spirits in order not to entertain the wrong kind of strangers.

Children, in this long letter of experiences, I have shared many ways in which our heavenly Father moves in situations to meet needs and give answers, directions, or help in various circumstances. The Word of God is a mighty tool as we sojourn through life. God keeps his promises. The name of Jesus is another mighty instrument that is available at all times. Angels, people, and finances give help along the way. God can and may use time and weather to move on situations, and the list goes on. Some of the greatest help in the time of need is the "Blood of Jesus, the Lamb slain from the foundation of the world." The Blood of Jesus is the only thing that can cleanse us from our sins. However, we can apply the Blood of Jesus in any situation for our protection. Let me explain.

A number of years ago, Carl and I were going to a waterbed factory to pay for the purchase of our bed that we had ordered built. The owners of the establishment had informed us at the time that we placed the order to always call ahead before coming in. They had a large male German shepherd guard dog, and when customers came, they put it away. I forgot to call ahead. Carl and I walked through the iron gate into a large fenced area. We were halfway in the yard when this large shepherd met us. I suddenly remembered the instructions, but it was too late. Neither Carl nor I said a word, not to the dog, nor to each other. I began to think on the "Blood of Jesus." I thought of nothing else. Soon we were safe inside the establishment. I thought that the lady was literally going to have a heart attack. For the next twenty minutes, she grilled us on how we got past the guard dog. Carl later shared with me that he too thought on nothing but the Blood of Jesus.

Children, as your daily attire, stayed clothed in the armor of God. Keep the Blood of Jesus applied to your daily lives always. This will keep you fit for heaven or earth, live or die.

There is another dramatic event that is so touching it continues to portray the heavenly Father's great love and concern for His children.

I was saying my prayers before retiring for the night. I had a desire and a request to the Lord as I prayed. "Heavenly Father, I love you. I thank you for your many blessings; you've been so good to all of us. Father, I desire to send Karen my daughter a dozen long-stem red roses and to sign them, 'Love, Jesus.' I want her to know how much you love her. Father, you know that we are in a transition time and finances are low. I cannot afford roses right now. Would you help me to be able to do this for Karen?

"There are people who do not know that you exist, Father. They send their daughters roses frequently. You said if I would ask, that you would do it. I'm asking, Father. Thank you. Amen."

I prayed this prayer about nine o'clock at night and got

into bed. The next morning around eight o'clock the phone rang. It was Karen. "M-o-t-h-e-r, I know that it was you. What did you do that for?" "Do what?" I asked.

"Mother, you know what you did; no one but you would do a thing like that." "Like what?" I asked again.

"I was hardly out of bed when twelve long-stem red roses were delivered to my door. They were signed, 'Love, Jesus.' I know that it was you, Mom. Fess up." "Karen, I did not send you any roses. My budget will not permit me to do that." By this time I am weeping, praising, "Thank you, Jesus!"

"Karen, last night before I went to bed, I asked Jesus to help me send you a dozen long-stem red roses. I wanted to sign them, 'Love, Jesus.' " Finally I was able to convince her that it was not I. We thanked and praised our heavenly Father together.

Karen has a son who was born with the cord around his neck twice. He was born dead but was revived. . . . She and her husband lived in such trauma and sorrow. That is why I wanted her to know how much God loves her.

To this day neither Karen nor I know who or how the roses got delivered to her door that morning. The time frame of their delivery is phenomenal. We do know that God answered prayer to the exact sender.

I signed these writings, "Love, Mom," but Jesus wrote them in red and signed them a long time ago, Love Jesus to all of the world. You can read them in John 3:16 (KJV).

Love, Mom